A Path Through Ohio

A Cyclist's Guide to the Ohio to Erie Trail

Second Edition

Mark J. Looney

All information presented in this book is for general knowledge and does not constitute direct advice for your own health and safety while enjoying bicycle travel. As with any physical activity, please consult your doctor before engaging in cycle travel. This book presents directional advice from maps obtained by the referenced organizations at the time of this trip, since this writing there have been and will continue to be improvements to each trail system. I strongly recommend using the web sites located in the reference section of this book to obtain the current revision of each document before venturing on your own. The ideas in this book are based on my own research and many years of cycling experience along the trail and open road. This work constitutes a good faith effort to connect the sound bites of history that have been selected for your travels through Ohio. I hope you find this story informative and inspires you to take up your bike and explore Ohio.

ISBN 978-0-9982204-1-3

Ohio to Erie Trail State Bike Route 1

Introduction

In 1980, as a young and terribly inexperienced solo bike rider clad in sneakers, cut-off sweats and hauling a bunch of camping gear strapped to a cheap bike rack, I took off across the country on a 10-speed bicycle. The trip resulted in an adventure chock-full of memories and fulfilled goals. After a three-decade hiatus, the reasons not to venture out on the open road had become fewer and further between, resulting in a desire to re-experience the freedom and spontaneity that only solo bicycle travel seems to satisfy. Exploring untraveled roads rekindled a vaguely familiar mix of feelings including the determination to set and complete a goal or the fascination of exploring secondary back roads or the adventure of meeting new people and sharing in their ideas. Now in my 50s, I have arguably slowed down physically (and maybe even mentally, so my friends say). An old, familiar twitch had grown from inside and it was now upon me to re-experience the thrill and enjoyment that bicycle touring once brought.

The idea for a trip across Ohio started with a small article written by Susan Glaser and published in the *Cleveland Plain Dealer* in April of 2014. The article celebrated the opening of the Ohio to Erie Trail, (OTET) which had been in development since 1991. The cross-state path was the brainchild of Ed Honton, a Franklin County Engineer and the first appointed Bicycle Coordinator for the Ohio State Department of Transportation. What started as a series of independent trails throughout the state now are connected into a bike path corridor through Ohio. Today, the popular OTET is managed and promoted by the *Ohio to Erie Fund* and its Board of Directors. The announcement of a four-segment bike ride across the state of Ohio was just the motivation I needed to return to the roads by bike.

Through the significant efforts of the *Ohio to Erie Bike Trail Fund* and the Ohio Department of Transportation, a 326-mile multi-use path across the state had been created. As County, State and National *Rails to Trails* organizations have been growing in the past decade, so too has the interest to unify and connect trails between states. For this reason, the OTET has recently received the distinguished honor of becoming the first state bike route for Ohio, State Bike Route 1. And just to confuse things just a little bit more, it has also been designated as part of United States Bike Route; USBR 21, by the American Association of State Highway and Transportation Officials, (AASHTO) and the National Rails to Trails arm of this network program. Honton's inspiring vision of a cross-Ohio trail will one day become part of a much larger trail system extending to Atlanta, Georgia.

In the First Edition of *A Path Through Ohio, 2014* my aspirations were to introduce the reader to the rich history as seen by a soloist biker's eyes. For years, I had used the independent paths of the Little Miami Scenic Trail to run or explore in the Dayton area. I had no idea they would eventually form an interconnected trail system free of most automobile traffic. The 88 counties comprising the state of Ohio include a range of geographic diversity from the shores of Lake Erie through the rolling hills of Holmes County from the significant grades of southeastern Ohio to the state's southern border formed by the Ohio River. Though only portion of the State's 88 counties is traveled, the Ohio to Erie Trail cuts across the state's heartland, opening itself up to entertain the curious mind and to experience a sampling of its terrain, its culture, and its history–a wonderful experience on two wheels. In Xenia, the trail also connects to the western branch of the Erie Canal along the Miami River, and appropriately named the Miami Valley Bikeways. The combined paths offer more than 400-miles of automobile-free space to travel.

Ohio has a rich history with indigenous Indian tribes dating back centuries before the European and American interests moved west across the country. *A Path Through Ohio* introduces the reader not only to the state's topography but also to its cultural history. During my travels, I traversed the same land used by many Native American tribes including the Chippewa, the Delaware, the Miami, and the Shawnee. My interest in Ohio's state history was sparked many years ago when reading Allen W. Eckert's, *The Frontiersmen*. This tale of a lesser-known (except perhaps to Ohioans and historians) pioneer named Simon Kenton and his acquaintance, the more popular Daniel Boone, became my source of inspiration and reading for many years. Together with the chronicle of the short-lived Erie Canal system, and the introduction of the locomotive, Ohio's was and continues to be a source of many forms of travel. The history along the OTET does not end with its frontier developments either, there are numerous points of interest of which Ohio played a pivotal role during our nations great civil unrest and the emancipation of slavery along the Underground Railroad. There are two Union, Civil war encampments positioned along the same escape routes used by the runaway slaves just a few years earlier. Also woven into Ohio's history and the bike path were once dominant industries now reduced to rubble. Always a curiosity for me was the background to their rise and decline. The path and its surrounding areas has seen so much history that it was simply a challenge to select which stories to keep within the scope of this writing.

This first-hand narration of two-wheel travel through the state allows the reader an opportunity to visualize and ride along and experience the landscape that was integral to Ohio's values from the saddle view of a bicycle. It is an escape from today's 9-to-5 (and often grinding), lifestyle to enjoy the random acquaintance of people that form Ohio's unique culture. Equipped with three decades of physical training and camping experience, my open-road and back country survival skills have been assembled into a literary package that may help prepare you for an experience that you can call your own. Within this writing, you will find a layering of what I discovered to be my guiding principles of bike travel, my road rules. Experiences collected from solo cycle travel, backpacking and in some cases from the world of marathon training; another hobby of sorts. These personal discoveries are provided as stories within the overall travels through Ohio in hopes that it smooths the path for your own travels. *Looney's Road Rules,* is a lighthearted way to share with others the skills I obtained and the lessons I learned through years of adventure travel. Each has a deeper meaning for me and, in many cases, was something learned the hard way. It is my desire that these will conjure up your own personal experiences, which could then become your list.

Now in its second edition, A Path Through Ohio takes a different perspective of bike travel that extends beyond the seasoned wit and wisdom of a sometimes-sardonic solo traveler. Some may call it a long bike ride or the overused "journey", and then again others may think of it as an adventure. Out of curiosity I looked up the term adventure in the dictionary and found an adventure to include: "an exciting or unusual experience that usually involves risks". Knowing some of the risks of distance cycling, I was thinking this was an adventure with many layers.

In this second edition, I travel the OTET the opposite direction from the 2014 trip. Enjoying the scenery from a different perspective. Now starting from its southern terminus in Cincinnati along the Ohio River and ending at the water's edge of Lake Erie in Cleveland. Added to the second edition are mileage charts, improved town and city descriptions, more historic references and of course more personalities adding to the rich and textured diversity of people you may one day encounter along the trail. Adding to the fun was a larger group of 35 bike riders, mostly from Ohio and a few from out of state. In September of 2017, we left from the abutments of the John Roebling Bridge in Cincinnati that resulted in a much different riding experience. It enabled me to meet many of the individuals responsible for the development and maintenance of the trail system now called the OTET. Central to this organization is Tom Moffett, President of the OTET Fund, along with a Board of Directors each representing one of the 22 trail systems and Counties that the conjoined OTET represent. The trail system for all intents and purposes is complete, and as with any growing organization there are plenty of opportunities to improve. Property disputes, sign placement, maintenance and funding for new and enhanced trails are constantly a focus for the OTET Fund. During the 2017 trip, I rode along a fresh two-week-old layer of tarmac representing a seven-mile enhancement through Holmes county and some of Ohio's pristine hardwood forests unencumbered by highway noise and county crossroads. This being an example of the direct improvements that are underway here on the OTET.

In this second edition, you will find a greater variety of services as the communities surrounding the trail are increasing their support of the OTET. Cities and states have long urged their residents to ride bicycles, as a healthy form of recreation and as a green alternative to driving. Now they're recognizing pedal power's economic potential. In Ohio, there are more and more trails being built with many connecting to the OTET. Whether you're new to riding bikes, or a seasoned veteran of bike touring, the time and resources has never been better to get out on the trail and ride a bike. There are many options to enjoying your bike. Many cyclists are riding out and back, point to point or stringing a series of day rides, some are even connecting pieces of the trail together and eventually completing the entire trail! The point is to get outside and enjoy the scenery, start a conversation with another, benefit from turning those pedals over and let the breeze remind you that your body is in motion and the excitement that two-wheel travel brings forward in your soul.

I hope you enjoy this book and I look forward to seeing you on the bike paths of Ohio.

Regards,
Mark Looney

Day One
Cleveland to Dalton, Ohio - 81 miles

Located on the shore of Lake Erie and the western side of Cleveland, OH is a beachfront city park called Edgewater. Within its boundaries is more than a mile of lake shoreline ranging from sandy beaches to rocky fishing coves and wide-open greenway's. This multi-use park commonly host's birthday parties, volleyball games and an occasional paraglider lifting off from the cliff's overlooking the shore. On a lazy sunny afternoon a variety of sailboats can be seen flirting with the wind from the overlooking embankment. Since the turn of the century; (1894) this park has been a popular recreational spot for many, and at one time boasted an old hotel on the sandy shores of its natural harbor. Today, Edgewater Park serves as the Trailhead for the Ohio To Erie Trail; commonly known as the OTET. A short commute from the Cleveland Bus Terminal, Train Depot or even the Cleveland Hopkins International Airport can place most travelers on its sandy beaches. An elegant new Pavilion on the shores of Erie carefully blends the openness of beach life with the sandstone and shale geology of the surrounding embankments. The Pavilion along with an associated shower house also serves as a convenient terminus for the trail. Popular to many who chose to ride the entire 326-mile trail system is the ceremonial "wheel dip" in Lake Erie and later Ohio's southern boundary, the Ohio River in Cincinnati.

For a number of years since moving to Cleveland I had started to ride my bike more often, taking it for a quick 15 to 20-mile spin in the nearby parks. The next year I joined a local bike shop's club rides. The miles started to grow along with my confidence to return to cycle touring as a less impactful option to my fading running. I was a career marathoner and triathlete for the past 35 years, the cumulative impact that running on the roads had on my body had begun to take a toll and I realized that my running career was coming to an end. After numerous x-rays and a half dozen doctor visits over as many years, it became clear to me that I was suffering from a degenerative, arthritic hip. This condition was already slowing me as a competitor and was a constant reminder of this physical deterioration each time I laced up for a run. I knew I would have to make some lifestyle changes soon if I were to stay physically fit.

Some 30 years ago distance cycling had been a complimentary form of exercise I used to augment my running and triathlon racing. The renewed excitement of the wind hissing through my helmet; the exhilaration of blood coursing through my legs; the regaining of my high school metabolism and my curiosity of what lies over the next hill or turn all conspired to reawaken my senses to an old friend, the bicycle.

Gradually running was being replaced with cycling and now I was considering multi-day bicycle trips, otherwise known as cycle touring. Pick a destination on a map, add some elements of the unknown like camping, unpredictable weather, or a chance encounter with a stranger, and you end up with a good old-fashioned adventure just waiting to unfold. The Cleveland Metroparks became a wonderful training ground and set the stage for the ride across the state of Ohio.

Standing at the front door of my home, I noticed an uncommon coolness in the lakeside air. A seagull screeched by as a light summer breeze gently blew southeast from the Lake Erie shore. A perfect sunny day with wispy clouds brushed over a tapestry of blue sky was on tap for the first day's ride.

A short commute by bike from my residence to Edgewater Park was required before officially starting on the OTET. My wife Laurie and daughter Erin saw me off on this morning with a familiar look on their face that seemed to say "You're doing this for what reason?" "Don't forget to call me", was the last thing I heard as I rolled down the driveway. Taking some familiar backroads, I weaved my way to Edgewater Park and the Lake Erie shoreline.

For a city park, Edgewater has a unique openness and "big sky" feel as opposed to some of its inland sister parks forming the

Cleveland Metropark system. On a good day you can catch a beautiful sunrise over the city skyline and a soothing sunset over the western end of Lake Erie. From the Pavilion on the beach and a bike trail label (a green oval with a white silhouette of a bicycle and the number "1") I knew I was in the right spot to start this adventure. Also, this was a great place to snap a picture of my bike's front wheel in Ohio's northern border. A ceremonial opportunity that many riders take advantage of when traveling the OTET and State Bike Route 1.

Wrapping my head around the adventure I was about to embark on I take a last look of at vast lake and push off with the first inertial heave of the bike. Heading south out of the park towards the sandstone bridge and the Route 2 underpass I follow the bike path turning left at the intersection. And of course I encounter the first hill of the day a short mile from the lake. With inclining switchbacks on the bike path I approach an ornate mosaic entrance tunneling under a railroad bed and tracks above. Passing through the other side of the tunnel was an equally impressive mosaic work on the retaining wall surrounding the tunnel. Images of bicycles laid out in color tiles with a backdrop of the lake. At the top of the climb I notice beginning stages the future bike path which will take a less congested route through the trendy area know as Gordon Square. However, for the time being the bike path places me suddenly into the city life of Cleveland and its surrounding suburbs on 65th street. The stark contrast from lakeside air to gritty streets caused me to pause a bit while I reassessed my now urban environment.

Navigating through any city for the first time can be intimidating for a cyclist, Cleveland is no exception. Turning left onto Franklin Avenue are signs of a city on the move. Run-down factories give way to vibrant revitalization with portions of new construction and back again. The intertwined trendy boutiques and restaurants give the feeling of a gritty city making a resurgence to its glory days. As the early 7:30 start placed me smack in the middle of the city's morning traffic, I found this an uncomfortable beginning for a free spirit, looking to hit the open road and trails. The bold, painted bike lines on the uneven cement and asphalt surface provided a clear path for a safe passage through the city and the traffic showed little objection to my presence. After a couple of miles, east on Franklin Avenue and a right turn onto West 25th street, I quickly spied the tower of the West Side Market which marks the site of the 100-year-old Farmer's Market. Stopping to take a picture of the Ohio State Historic Marker for the West Side Market I determined that I would photograph and catalog each marker I encounter on the OTET this became a source of curiosity throughout the ride. The results of which are summarized in the Appendix. Passing the Market immediately tickled my senses as the aroma of fresh bread, colorful fruit & vegetables, and the floral arrangements made it easy to see how, for decades, Clevelanders had been enticed to stop by and enjoy fresh and homegrown fare.

Just past the West Side Market and following a quick left turn onto Lorain Avenue, the Lorain-Carnegie Bridge can be seen crossing the Cuyahoga River and connecting Cleveland's west and east ends as it has since 1932. This iconic bridge was listed on the National Register of Historic Places in 1976 and is a fine example of an Art Deco truss bridge. The 43-foot sandstone pylons, known as the Guardians of Traffic, flank each end of the bridge, symbolizes the progress in transportation over the past decades. In the 1980s, the bridge was renamed the Hope Memorial Bridge to commemorate its stonemason, William Henry Hope, the man who carved these structures. He also happens to be the father of the popular 20th-century comedian, Bob Hope.

From the Lorain Avenue side of the West Side Market, I look for Abbey Avenue which is connected by Gehring Road, a stone's throw away. While on Abby for a short mile take a right onto 14th Street which leads the biker through the trendy Tremont neighborhood. Needing a break after navigating these first initial miles I ride up to a street side café, lean my bike against the old brick building and walk inside for a quick cup of joe and a pastry to go. Comically, I've only logged five miles and felt the need for a break. The well-worn wooden threshold was a sign this old shop had seen better days, but better yet it was a good indicator of the shops popularity. With a friendly smile from the barista and my drink in hand I headed outside to review my maps.

Back on my bike again I take a little extra time to explore Tremont, and the elevated views from its embankments I could catch brief glimpses of the Cuyahoga River Valley between trees and buildings. For decades, this was and remains the heart of the city's industry, allowing large freighters to pass the winding river making deposits of ore before returning back to the lake. However, amongst all this industry, Tremont is a hilltop oasis that secludes itself from much of the noise and industry below. When I traveled in 2014 the deconstruction of the old I-90 Bridge was all around. Iron girders were strewn on either side of the river like an erector set project gone bad. Today, the large span across the Cuyahoga to the other side of the valley is an impressive engineering feat to behold.

Leaving the quaint neighborhood of Tremont and its perch along the embankments of the Cuyahoga River, the bike path takes the rider down a generously sweeping turn and through a short tunnel that then opens up to a strip mall called, The Steel Yard Commons. If you're in need of supplies like food or water before exiting Cleveland's outer city limits, this is your last convenient stop before traveling some of the longer stretches of reclaimed green space.

Riding south on bike path out of the city's heavy industry lies the Harvard Avenue A left and turn and a quarter mile on Harvard Avenue will place the rider in front of the Harvard Avenue Trailhead. Near the Trailhead entrance is the old Alcoa Aluminum Foundry. Some interesting displays of wheel forgings and other product produced by Alcoa can be found outside along the trail for those interested. Soon the Alcoa plant and the remnants of Cleveland's heavy industry are transformed into miles of beautiful greenway for many to enjoy. Alongside the path at a safe distance are the busy streets of Independence, with historical train bridges passing overhead and remnants of the Erie Canal within a stone's throw. Occasionally, a grey stealthy heron can be seen skillfully searching for its next meal amongst the lily pads.

As I get comfortable with my surroundings and the bike wheels start spinning with little effort I start thinking about some of my earlier experiences as a young student in high school. Easily, my memory goes back to a time when I had the first notion that this long-distance bike riding would ingrain itself in my subconscious thoughts. It all started in July of 1980, a chance encounter with a solo cross-country cyclist became the start of my quest to do the same in 1983. To ride a bicycle was not a particularly cool thing back in those days. Most of my friends from Webster, New York, where I spent my formative years, were muscle car fans. A favorite was the Ford Mustang. To this day, these gear heads have an encyclopedic memory of each car's output and component origination. For me, an interest in exploring the physical limits of human endurance through distance running outweighed the desire for horsepower by mechanical strength (although, I must admit that a '66 ragtop Mustang does sit in my garage today). As a young man, the ride across the United States became a dream pinned by a successive series of improvements in physical and mental preparation.

After reading Peter Jenkins' bestseller, *A Walk Across America,* I became intrigued with the solitary lifestyle of a solo traveler. In Jenkins' case, it was a backpacker traveling over 5,000 miles on foot. Employing the patience of a marathoner and the self-reliance of a solo traveler, I took off on my own coast-to-coast mission to explore the country. Over the long, quiet miles, I started to form my thoughts of personal conduct while on the road. The underlying theme of endurance sport is learning to endure. In order to endure, one must learn to enjoy from within the activity in which they have engaged. Over time, these ideas evolved into a code of conduct I now refer to as "Looney's Road Rules". One of my favorite road rules is to find a song that reflects my mood and use that song to help motivate me to ride strong.

Road Rule Number One
Start every day with a song.

"Begin the day with a friendly voice, a companion unobtrusive, plays that song that's so elusive, And the magic music makes your morning mood" (Rush, Permanent Waves).

I am a big fan of starting each day with the right attitude in order to gain peak performance from my body. Whether it is the ride into the office or shaking off last night's thundershower while holed up in a tent, the new day brings opportunities to meet new people or to explore one of earth's treasures. As any good athlete prepares for an event, the warm-up is the tool of choice to stretch the body and warm the muscles in preparation for the event. Similarly, the mind needs to warm up. Positive platitudes, visualization exercises, and music are the brain's favorite tools for programming. Although we're not all athletes, starting the day with a positive outlook allows the rider to hop on that saddle just one more time, shake off that cold morning chill, and start churning those pedals to the cadence of a familiar drum beat.

I once had the opportunity to watch the Team USA sprinters warm up for the day's practice at the US Olympic Training Center in Chula Vista, California. From a distance, I watched them jog through their drills on the 400-meter track. At the near end of the beautifully surfaced track was a five-story tower that supported a viewing box and a significant speaker system. As the sprinters concluded their warm-up drills, one came to the tower and blared two audio tracks. The first was a tape from an Olympic stadium with crowd noise as background and the other was the runner's favorite rap music. Inspired by this music, the team went to work immediately.

Each morning before the sun casts its rays upon the road or the grind of another long day is to begin, there is a need to jump-start the solitary spirit of a solo traveler. The best songs are ones that pop into your head without effort. It may be a lyric or a verse that has grabbed the wandering attention of an unsuspecting moment in the past. Often times, it's associated with a strong memory or emotion. In either case, this becomes the cadence and rhythm that encourages the mind and body to work together as one. This road rule was created out of necessity to soften the long hours in the saddle. And, it fills the void created by the lack of human conversation while traveling companionless.

The journey's first song is by an old favorite band of mine called Foreigner. With its lead singer, Lou Graham a hometown favorite of Rochester, New York a vague memory of the lyrics began to cogitate in my mind. "There's a mountain I must climb, feels like a weight upon my shoulder". Gradually, the full song, *I Want to Know What Love Is,* came together in my mind. These opening lyrics described the mood and tone I was feeling while on this latest adventure.

Riding the OTET brought back the exhilaration of being on the open road again with my bicycle. It also brought back some anxiety from my cross-country trip of 1983. As young man thousands of miles from home, the raw emotion of "what the hell are you getting yourself into" was replaced by a calm sense of confidence and determination. I have trained well and hell, I've done this kind of thing before. The bike, weighing in at an easy 35-pounds, is further burdened by an additional 40-pound load of gear and food on the back of the bike. Despite this load, the bike was manageable. As a matter of science, a fully loaded bike is known to reduce the rider's efficiency by up to 20 percent as compared to an unencumbered road bike. My plan was to not expect more than 75 miles per day.

As the feelings of excitement and the prospect of this new adventure began to morph into a business-like cadence on the pedals, so too did the feeling of being exposed to the outdoors and a sense of unbridled exploration. The mid-morning sun on my face, the smell of fresh-cut grass, and the sound of pea gravel grinding underneath my tires all heightened the senses. With a modest 20 miles from this morning's start my Cateye® speedometer is reading a comfortable 13 to 15 miles per hour. Passing through the city of Independence I encounter a pair of white suspension bridges that conveniently put me over some of the cities congested traffic below, each in short succession from each other, force me to shift gears on my bike and climb the short distance and coast down the back side with ease. Within a couple of miles, I look up to the sky and see the I-77 Valley View Bridge, ushering the city's busy traffic hundreds of feet above the valley floor. Another short mile away I am startled by a much lower clearance, a steel girder almost within reach of my extended hand which signals the crossing of Rockside Road above. From this bridge, the trail ushers the rider into Ohio's history of canal life beginning in the 1820s. It also marks a pleasant change in path surface conditions as asphalt gives way to a curving boardwalk underneath Rockside Road and emerges into a crushed limestone pathway that replicates the old horse trodden paths used nearly 200 years ago. For the next 20 miles, riders are treated to the firm and forgiving trail bed that closely reproduces the backdrop our early pioneers used to transport their products to market centuries ago.

Alongside the canal is the active Cuyahoga Rail System serving as a reminder of the region's transportation progression that sadly led to the end of the Erie Canal system. Displacing long boat for locomotive engine the short-lived 30-year use of the canal saw its demise as track was laid in the same river valley. Conveniently located for riders of all skill is the Rockside Train Depot, representing the northern endpoint of a scenic path through the Cuyahoga National Park for both rider and pedestrian. For a nominal fee both rider and bicycle can be commuted to numerous destination points along the train line and bike path south towards Akron. The Towpath (bike path) runs side-by-side with the canal which shares a common heritage of moving travelers. What was most surprising about today's ride was the ease in pedaling and smoothness of the road surface offered by the crushed limestone. When riding on a traditional path, a rider's undercarriage (my term for a saddle-and-rider interface, also known as the butt, tush, posterior, or derriere) may suffer some discomfort resulting from traveling over occasional bumps and exposed roots on the path. This discomfort can be alleviated somewhat with fat, 38mm road tires. On this particular section of trail, however, after a mere 20 minutes of traversing the comparatively smooth limestone paths, I believe that even the inexperienced rider will find this an enjoyable surface to travel.

As I passed through the city of Independence, there were numerous trailside markers providing details of historically significant communities and a settler's lifestyle along this important waterway. Located just five miles south of Cleveland, this long-inhabited area served as the crossroads for nomadic Indians who roamed the area along the well-established trails of the Muskingum and the Mahoning. Early settlers originally named "Independence" as a region in which indigenous Indians of the area and pioneers alike would agree to contentedly coexist in the Cuyahoga River Valley allowing for each to hunt, farm, and gain vital resources for survival. With the development of the Erie Canal through this area in the 1850s, the early settlers were replaced by a more industrious brand of settler who used the waterway as a means to move produce and highly valued sandstone used for gristmills. This commerce ultimately placed Independence on the map of modern importance. The trail offers many opportunities to carefully examine the remains of locks used to control the water flow and depth, which allowed the long boats to travel in either direction. In some cases, the lock keepers' residence may be found nearby. As with much of Ohio's transportation history, trails gave way to canals, which were shortly followed thereafter by rail. Nearly 400 years later, Independence continues to serve as a major crossroad for commerce as the intersections of I-77 and I-480 take travelers through this historic region. Meanwhile, on bike, the passage of history unfolds while riding along some of the original paths created by our ancestors.

As the trail continues south, and reaches the town of Peninsula a distinct change in the scenery is seen with mature tree coverage replacing the open grasslands. This makes for a pleasant canopy and protection from the sun. While passing through the trails, I soon found myself in the middle of a group ride for children sponsored by Century Cycles, a local bicycle shop. Watching the little daredevils weave in and around my "big rig" brought a grin to my face as I was reminded of a more youthful time. This young bike enthusiast left no mud puddle untouched, nor was a child left without a mud stripe up his backside. The inquisitive kids quickly moved to one side or the other of the trail as I gently announced my riding up through the rear of their pack. Having survived my encounter with the younger set and without significant fanfare or any national park signage, I discovered that I was entering the Cuyahoga Valley National Park.

Arriving at the small trailside stop of Boston Mills, I came upon a quaint farm home now turned Visitor Center for the National Park Service. An old historic tavern with an inviting wraparound porch and white rocking chairs facing the trail created in me a certain temptation for a seat of a different kind. While peering through the floor-to-ceiling pane glass windows, an intriguing landscape model of a nearby lock and long boat construction business was found. Upon further investigation inside the Visitor Center, I happened upon a reduced-size, cut-away model of a long boat. The cut-away exposed the meticulous mortise-and-tenon joinery necessary to create these 90-foot long passenger and freight vessels.

Shortly after leaving Boston Mills, I encountered a farm stand. In reality, it was more like an open-door farmer's market with a wide range of fruits and vegetables. Everything was fresh and colorful. With little thought this became my first official lunch stop of the trip. In front of the market was a parking area for a spin-off business of "try and like" wooden lawn gliders for sale. As I was gliding back and forth, eating fresh peaches in the sun, it became apparent that the Amish carpenters, with their famed woodworking skills, were onto a brilliant marketing technique using the proximity of the towpath as a means of commerce for their products. The gliders were so comfortable and an easy distraction for the weary biker. After lunch, the miles started to roll by pretty easily along the crushed gravel path. The midday sun tried to pierce through the heavy forest canopy with selected leaves exploding in color as the backlight of the sun struggled to reach the ground. Hats off to the National Park Service for their meticulous care of the trail and surrounding beauty. After passing through Cleveland and now being immersed in the natural beauty of the National Park, the perfect weather conditions, the full enjoyment of riding through this outdoor treasure was becoming a reality of the Ohio to Erie Trail.

While riding through the National Park the small and inconspicuous community of Peninsula is a modest 13-mile ride from the Rockside Train Station, providing service to travelers of many types. It is also a popular stopping point for those wishing to extend their travel range throughout the park by train. I was pleasantly impressed to find a bike shop in this outpost town in the event that repairs and adjustments might be needed. There are also a couple of options to refuel and hydrate at one of the local establishments. With the bike path now tied to the Summit County Park system trail markers on the OTET promote primitive camping for those who need a place to pitch a tent, running water and restroom for the night. Approximately 26 miles from the lake by bike path look for a tepee marker on a fixed wooden post. A short 100-yard walk will give way to an open grassy space with a sign-in station if your intention is to stay overnight.

Gradually, the signs for exiting the national park gave way to the city of Akron. Now in the outskirts of northern Akron, frequent street crossings provided clues that the uninterrupted crushed gravel pathway was soon to end. While passing through the city of Akron, I was impressed with the care taken to mark the path with a red dashed line for those of us just passing through town. This minimized the confusion of intersecting bike paths and co-use streets as bike lanes. The path carefully passes through the city and wraps around the outfield of the minor league baseball stadium, which is home to the Akron Rubber Ducks, an AA feeder team to the Cleveland Indians. Clearly, this was a well laid-out city path designed to showcase the city's offerings and beauty. The southern part of Akron continued to display its impressive trail way through the use of carefully constructed boardwalks along Summit Lake and the interconnecting waterways forming the Portage Trail System by way of canoe. The informational placards posted along the trail provide a deep history of the region's importance. This was a common start and end-point for an eight-mile long portage used by the Cuyahoga and Tuscarora Indians for seasonal hunting. Though a north-south passage to the Ohio River was desired, the topography of the region and increased elevation caused these ancient travelers to carry their gear from one point to another for eight miles to reach their destination. Likewise, the engineers of the early 1820s recognized the same problem although their solution was a bit different. They chose to dig the canal deeper and developed locks to artificially raise the water level, allowing boats to pass through the higher elevation.

After passing through Summit Lake on the expansive boardwalk I took note of the life sized Woodland Indian statue at the Northern terminus of the Summit County Bike Trail. The Indian carrying his canoe, provides a view of the arduous journey performed seasonally to access fertile hunting grounds hundreds of years ago. After reading the historical marker, I could not help but feel being drawn back in time as the bike path retraced the ancient trail used by these early inhabitants. The only difference was that I was going to roll along the trail with my gear lashed to my bike, rather than carrying it on my back. Modernization has its benefits. As the miles rolled by, numerous locks most in disrepair, became a good reason to take pause and note the manual labor that was required to dig the miles of waterway.

Traveling another 17 miles from Akron the rider will be pleasantly surprised as the city of Canal Fulton emerges through the forested path. The path takes riders through a small city park with shops and restaurants backed up against the canals edge as it takes on the buzz of an old canal port settlement. Crossing the canal on Cherry Street will quickly usher the interested rider onto North Canal Street. The City of Canal Fulton retains much of its historic feel as the towpath parallels the main street through the city. If time is available, this quaint town atmosphere is worth a visit to explore further. Including rides on the longboat called the Saint Helena, III, offered by the Canal Fulton Heritage Society. Draft horses are fed and maintained along the towpath and are interchanged as each tour down the river and back is completed. I had an opportunity to observe some of the logistical challenges encountered after some 150 years of technological advances. With a dozen or more guests fully loaded on the reconditioned St. Helena, three young men–the operators–struggled mightily to turn the boat around in a tight portion of the canal in order to load the next set of guests. Against my nature to pitch in and help, I chose to stay in the background and not get recruited. Meanwhile, as the struggle to straighten the boat continued, the pole-men used a combination of ropes, pole pushing, and body weight to gradually find a wider notch in the canal in which to swing the boat 180 degrees, allowing the guests to disembark. The entire operation of turning the vessel lasted well over 45 minutes, much too long for this casual observer. The park also contained a dry-docked long boat, allowing visitors to inspect the workmanship of these antique vessels. It was well worth the stop to gain a perspective of the early freight and mass transit system at work. At least no one had to portage his vessel through this area.

Leaving Canal Fulton and continuing on, I parked my bike at Lock 4 with a historic marker. While taking pictures for my research, I started a conversation with an older lady and her grandson. She was very interested in the ride to Cincinnati. We talked about common points of interest along the trail and she told me how she would like to "take up her bike" and ride the trail someday. I encouraged her to plan a ride with her grandson as a bonding opportunity.

While standing next to the brick Lock Tenders house I read a couple of historic markers nearby and discovered this lock to be the last functioning lock between Cleveland and Portsmouth, OH. At one time (one hundred and forty-six) such locks controlled the three hundred mile water highway. Built originally in 1827 the Erie Canal met its demise because of the incumbent rail line and the flood of 1913 which put an end to its usefulness. During its time of operation, the canal fueled the early growth of the cities of Akron, Massillon and Canal Fulton.

Reading my map, I knew Massillon lay a short eight miles further down the towpath trail. Entering the Sippo Valley Trail, another rider passed me by. All I saw was a white sunbonnet, rolled up jeans, and an obnoxious bike bell that was used liberally to clear the trail. I nearly jumped out of my skin when the rider lay on the bell as she passed by. I eventually caught up with her and we engaged in a long game of leapfrog; passing and re-passing each other numerous times. I introduced myself after the second pass. We rode together long enough that Betty had the time to explain, before she sped off ahead of me, that she was an active 70-year-old woman on a mission. I liken this to old-fashioned speed dating. As this comical parade continued for many miles, I was curious about her motivation to ride so fast so I pressed my pace again and finally caught back up to her.

I asked, "Where are you headed?" With brevity of words and a sense of determination, she said that she wanted to get to McDonald's before it closed because they had a sale on chocolate-dipped ice cream cones for 50 cents. It was over 30 years ago that I remember devouring two to three ice cream cones at a time from Mickey D's while on my cross country bike trip. It always made for a great afternoon treat while pedaling around. As I was trying to catch old Betty and also trying to catch my breath she turned off the path. As she reached the bridge rampart to Lincoln Way into Massillon, she gave me a "beauty queen" wave goodbye and she was off to McDonalds. There was another departure of sorts as the bike path turns away from the Tuscarawas River and takes a more westerly tact into the Sippo Valley region.

Riding through the Sippo Valley the towpath rises above the lower floodplain providing a visual perspective as a once prosperous farm land. I was reminded by local legend of the native Indians that inhabited the areas centuries ago. The Delaware tribe once used the Tuscarawas River, meaning "open mouth" and an ancient buffalo trace as its source of travel for years. The very path your bike travels today has its origins of what was once known as the "Great Trail" later used by pioneers to connect Fort Pitt (Pittsburg) to Fort Detroit as part of the western expansion.

Located right alongside the trail is a conveniently located bike shop called Ernie's; a father and son partnership perfectly situated at the Trailhead to take care of any bike needs you may have as you continue your bike travels. Make sure to stop in and say hi, to either Ernie, tell him Mark sent you!

The day was pushing towards four in the afternoon and I had hit my self-imposed, first day limit of 75 miles. In a way, this was a physical self-discovery experiment as I had not been on a loaded bike for many years and was not looking to push the limits of my physical capability. Knowing the city of Massillon had numerous options for overnight lodging I felt comfortable with riding further south on the trail and looking for a camping location, which is my natural preference. As 75 miles crept to 80, I was starting to feel the fatigue of a good day's effort turning into an exhausting long day and found myself anxious to find a quiet spot along the trail to open my tent for the evening. I passed a couple of beautiful, man-made lakes, each one very enticing for a dip. One pond was particularly inviting and had a fire pit and camp right by the trail. At the opposite end of this large acreage was a dog kennel business with an attached cabin. As I pulled alongside the pond to wash the days salt off my face, I noticed the kennel owner staring at me from her backyard deck. Another biker passing by saw the possible conflict and suggested I knock on the door and ask if a pitched tent at the far end of this beautiful spot would be allowed.

Trekking back a quarter of a mile, I had an uneasy feeling. The dogs in the kennel, clearly aware of my presence, got excited and I anticipated that the owner was ready for me. She answered my knock on the front door whereupon I politely complimented her on the property and described the nature of my travels. I asked if it would be acceptable for me to set up a tent at the far end of the pond. Unfortunately, I received a firm response of "I don't feel comfortable with that". Then she started quizzing me on my bike trip; where did I start from, how far had I travelled, who was I with and just generally poking at my cross-state story? Withering under her insistent cross-examination, I decided to give up on this spot. "Sometimes the juice is just not worth the squeeze" I thought to myself as I stepped off the porch and walked my bike back to the path.

When out of formal and approved camping options I will resort to a practice sometimes known as stealth camping. Carrying my gear, food and water on the bike allows me a degree of freedom to find a spot that is out of sight from human traffic. Provided a property is unmarked, I will unroll my tent and sleeping bag for a short night's rest. (This almost always means I am "out of town or on a rural road or bike path"). With a watchful eye for human traffic, hazards or in some way a disrupted night's sleep I will carefully make my selection and set-up camp. Along with this approach comes the added responsibility of ensuring no impact to the property, in any way. I have plenty of stories tenting in a perfectly serene setting only to find later that I am under a flight pattern of a nearby airport or visited by one of God's fuzzy critters; (racoons mostly) or epic mosquito infestation. These all become part of the experience stealth camping by bike if you choose to do so. With the popularity of the OTET it is equally easy to plan ahead and reserve a room at a nearby hotel or bed and breakfast for many destination points near the trail. This is also a way to stay immersed in the communities through which you travel. In the Appendix of this book is a listing of reasonable priced options for the do-it-yourself cyclist. Fortunately, for me a couple of miles down the path, I discovered a more hospitable site for camping. I pitched my tent in a clearing in the woods just a few feet from the path and started to wind down for the evening.

The first night's dinner was unappetizing as I unpacked an old "Meal Ready to Eat", also known quite efficiently as a MRE. This relic was left over from the Hurricane Katrina disaster in New Orleans back in 2005 and had been given to me by a Boy Scout friend who had volunteered there. The nine-year-old meal was carefully pulled apart and ingested for its calorie value only. The meal went down about as well as my initial effort for the first night's rest. The temperatures were mild as I sat down to summarize day one's fulfilling events. Interestingly, from my spot, I remained undetected as the evening trail walkers passed by me and my tent a short hundred feet from the trails edge.

Road Rule Number Two
Make a journal entry daily.

"There are a thousand thoughts lying within a man that he does not know till he takes a pen to write."
William Thackeray.

Summarize each day by making a conscious effort to capture the day's highlights or possibly the low points, the associated feelings, and the key learning. "Hell, I'll never do that again" may be just the note needed to prevent you from repeating the same mistake over. Each is a gem of an emotion to be recalled at a later point in time.

Journal writing in the privacy of your own space allows for free-flowing thoughts to be captured and, if desired, articulated more creatively at a later point. Surprisingly, some of my best moments of self-discovery and observation occur after a long day in the saddle with dinner in the tank and the evening sun fading on the horizon. Take the time to jot, draw, or scribble your likes and dislikes, how you felt, or maybe even a new bucket list idea. As Victor Frankl, a Holocaust survivor once wrote, "Writing allows us to free ourselves from our history". In part, I think he was trying to convey that the simple act of documenting our feelings allows us to move on in life to enjoy or suffer new feelings, making for a richer life experience.

Journaling after a long and eventful day was a practice my father insisted on many years ago. A practice I did not appreciated as a teenager biking across the county. But later as an adult it became a source of self-discovery. The thoughtful characterization of images and experiences has served as a gentle reminder of memorable moments from the road. Today's sunny day that seemed as if it would never end is one such memory. Remembering Road Rule Number Two and jotting some of my days experiences, I put down my pen around 8:30 and rested on top of my sleeping bag. The evening's mild air was a bit sticky from the day's lingering heat as I sat at the edge of my tent watching the colors of the bent wheat change hues of yellow, brown and gold with the gentle breeze passing through the field.

Day Two
Dalton to Mount Vernon - 76 miles

Early in the morning, a rustling in the brush and a snorting sound in the cool darkness piqued my awareness from within the frail protection of my tent. Half annoyed and half troubled, I stayed wrapped within the warmth of my sleeping bag as I made my observations. From outside my tent came another series of hoarse snorts that sounded like a disgruntled creature. Carefully listening to each strange noise, I gathered that whatever my morning visitor was, it was pacing back and forth to express its discontent. Now sitting upright, I planned my exit strategy in the event the creature took a more aggressive stance with me, its transgressor. While weighing my options, this experience reminded me of Road Rule Number Three.

Road Rule Number Three
Sleep with one eye open.

"You must stop and turn to face the dragon, to realize he is made of paper" (Chinese Proverb)

In today's world of verbal diarrhea on TV and bad news which sells best, our society is swept into a condition of fear; fear of walking the dog around the block; fear to go to the "east side" or "that" place. Fortunately, the cyclist does not run into this amped shock culture very often. For some, their fears are more founded in urban America rather than the woods of rural America. Yes, there are bears and deer and other wild critters out there that forage for food at night. In our mind's eye, we have a tendency to explode the snapping of a twig or a hearty snort of a buck as a threat and imminent danger that may be lurking in the dark. "Sleeping with one eye open" simply means to be aware of your surroundings and take appropriate precautions. Remove your food from your tent, don't camp near animal feces or tracks, and stay away from freshly dug holes or hollowed timber. Finally, when you first begin camping, you will likely only get partial sleep through most of your camp nights. These fears generally pass as your confidence grows with your capabilities and surroundings.

The camping part of adventure cycling is not for everyone. Consequently, there are many reasonable options to pursue. Plan ahead. Make sure your accommodations are confirmed the day before you arrive. Get cleaned up and sleep well. You will have the same challenges the next day as those who chose the ground upon which to sleep.

I have the greatest regard for those who have responded to the call of adventure. Those of you who have experienced this form of travel will likely attest that there is a vast network of bike shops that exhibit a general openness to help a fellow traveler. You're never really alone. The sandbox in which you play is just a little larger than most others.

With this disruptive and what I feared to be aggressive noise, I had to take stock of the situation and determine my next move. After careful thought, I deduced that I had pissed off some large animal, likely a deer or a cow. I decided that I would be best served to stay put and wait out the disruption through the balance of the morning while trying to get a little more shut-eye. Staring at the roof of my little pup tent and waiting for the sun to hit the treetops around me was not my idea of a good use of time. The pensive night's sleep left me with thoughts of the upcoming day's ride and caused me to rethink my decision to delay my departure. I decided to make an early and quick up-and-out after all. While rolling up my wet tent, I found a matted-down area of grass and some deer prints in the nearby mud. I guessed that this was likely the calling card of my early morning intruder. Maintaining a level of consciousness and awareness through the night is necessary when camping out of sight in unsecured locations. This practice is commonly known as stealth camping and should be used sparingly as conditions dictate.

Back on the bike path and pedaling by 6:40am, the familiar cadence of pedal spinning returned to its groove, the early sun's rays appeared over my shoulder. A surreal orange glow seeped through the trees, casting long shadows, which distorted the size of the trees and my bike. To my right were the iconic, rolling cornfields of Ohio with the hint of early morning dew over the field. The corn stalks were about four feet in height and glistened as the moisture on the leaves caught the sun's rays. A short time later, I came into Dalton and found a designated restroom in the village's vacated ballpark where I proceeded to indulge in a "bird bath" cleaning. Ah, the small pleasures of camping, I thought to myself.

Dalton before eight in the morning is a pretty uneventful sight apart from a possible racoon or other critter skittering across the street returning from its early morning forage. The sleepy village was unprepared for this morning traveler, and I had hoped to grab a quick bite or get a caffeine fix at the Dalton Dari-ette; located at the intersection of Mill Street and Route 30. This diner has been a fixture along this busy crossing since 1957, and has maintained its fifties styled hotdog and ice cream cuisine ever since. A great place for hungry cyclists, when their open for the season. Unfortunately, for me I was just too early and I had to take a pass on a proper breakfast. Having missed the day's breakfast and coffee, I wolfed down a handful of nuts and raisins and washed it down with water while riding through the deserted streets. I would later regret my decision to forgo a real breakfast, as the anticipated hills of Holmes County required more fuel than I had ingested.

For the next 15 miles the OTET returns to "surface roads"; (non-bike path) used by many modes of travel. These lightly traveled country roads belong to the Amish and generally contain challenging hills, which for me was a pleasant change from the normal flat bike path. The well-maintained houses are simple in design and portray a modest lifestyle. Dungarees and linens drying on the line, beautifully manicured and colorful front yard gardens, single-room schoolhouses, straw hatted bearded men walking the county roads with apparent determination and, of course, the black horse-drawn carriages all suggests a land frozen in time. Not that I look at laundry that often, I noticed something odd with the dungarees on the line, none of them had back pockets. This curiosity caused me to think of an old wives' tale about the Amish. "No pocket-no place for a lazy man's hands" was probably an extraction from the Bible that was turned into a matter of pragmatic adherence for their beliefs. On this day I hadn't seen anyone sitting on their hands, holding to the traditional belief that the Amish were rather industrious and practical people.

After an hour in the saddle since Dalton and having endured a couple of significant climbs, the hunger pangs were starting to return. In need of breakfast, I started searching for anything that appeared edible. Finally, I came across a "bump and dent" grocery store. As I entered the store, I noticed two impeccably dressed Amish children at the door. The boy was clad in blue jean overalls and the girl in a prairie dress. Both were shoeless and each was staring at me with a wide-eyed awe, almost as if I were the legendary Bigfoot sometimes reported to being seen in areas like this. I think we were each caught by surprise as the bohemian look of a cyclist generally tends to a more utilitarian look than with which most are comfortable. I was, of course, trying to assess the children's curiosity as they watched me peruse possible purchases in each of the half-dozen aisles of groceries. As I stepped forward to settle up for my purchase, the children were asked by a parent to step aside. This request was made in German, the primary language spoken in the Amish community. After a 20-minute shopping spree, my only purchase ended up being a six-pack of a popular brand-name breakfast drink that went down easily at first but later was found to have a terrible aftertaste, especially while drinking on the ride. I threw the remainder of the six-pack into my deep storage pannier. This unsatisfying concoction would eventually find its home in a convenient garbage can in the miles to come.

Meanwhile, the hills of Holmes County were gradually taking a toll on this loaded rider (85 pounds of bike and gear). By 11 am, I had covered only 20 miles. I was fortunate to enjoy favorable weather as I passed through this area. The day's temperature never exceeded 70 degrees, making for comfortable climbing up and down these wonderfully challenging hills. Along the way, I cracked a smile upon seeing a mother, in full Amish dress and with two young boys in tow, pushing a child in a baby carriage. Each boy would take his turn gleefully pulling the other in a handmade rickshaw styled as a black, horse-drawn carriage.

After a half day of travel in Holmes County, I grew wise to riding in the tracks of the horse-drawn buggies. These tracks, hardened from repeated contact with the buggy's steel-clad wheels, were much smoother than the rest of the trail and provided for much faster travel. And then there was the added challenge of avoiding the horse poop found between the paired carriage tracks. In my haste to find food I regrettably passed through the town of Apple Creek too quickly and later found out that I could have had a scrumptious cookie, pastry or other baked good at Troyer's Home Pantry. By this point in the travels the obvious symbiotic relationship of biking and eating is clear. Finally reaching the outskirts of Fredericksburg, the hills were starting to roll longer in my favor and I experienced the positive effects of Road Rule Number Four.

Road Rule Number Four
For every hill, there is an equal and opposite hill.

Having logged thousands of miles on bike and on foot, I have learned not to fight or become obsessed with the topography and the elements that Mother Nature and fate have put in my path. Standing in frustration at the base of a mountain or staring in the face of dark, foreboding clouds does not change the reality that you must either endure or go home. Rather, be prepared for the extremes and take action in advance to maintain reasonable comfort during tough times. For those of faith, these are the character-enriching experiences that you are in search of. It is God's way of shaping you to use your gifts, turning fear and humility into courage and accomplishment. The silver lining of each experience is that there is a downhill ride and a sunny side to each challenge. Recently, I met another distance cyclist who further characterized this Road Rule – when the wind is at your back make miles, when the wind is at your face take more photographs.

In this case, I had paid ahead with the hills for the entire morning and it was now time to reap the rewards of a nice, long glide into town. I came to the main intersection and the only traffic light in Fredericksburg. The early ride without breakfast had left me nearing the equivalent of caloric fumes. The unpleasant breakfast drink and trail mix reserves were an insufficient source of fuel to power up and down the Holmes County hills. A hard lesson to learn, again.

Road Rule Number Five
Know thy food and water needs.

Dietary and hydration concerns are always prevalent when one is exposed to the elements regardless of whether that exposure is just for hours or for trips lasting multiple days. Of the two, hydration is your number one concern in order to maintain proper body fluid levels. I have noticed that the combination of exposure and exercise can best be compensated with up to one liter per hour of water. When urinating, look for a clear fluid as an indication of your success. I also alternate water with sports drinks when on a particularity long grind to help replace lost electrolytes.

The calories burned (CB) during a long day's journey are also an important statistic to watch while actively riding. There are many calculators on the Internet that estimate the amount of CB during exercise. I suggest consulting your doctor before embarking on a journey. There are many variables that dictate your physiological needs on a given day. There is much more science behind the maintenance of your physical needs. As you become familiar with any form of distance exercise, be aware of your unique needs and replace calories and fluids regularly. I prefer ice cream any time the opportunity avails itself.

Plan ahead, know the distances between stops and if they are greater than a couple of hours, plan to pack extra reserves. Through force of habit, I generally carry two water bottles and energy bars as a reserve. Let your body be your first indicator to replace fluids and fuel.

As the creator of these invaluable road rules, you would think I would be more inclined to follow them but in this case, you would be wrong. I was definitely on Code Yellow and nearing Red with hunger pangs, light headedness and feeling a little disoriented. In years past, close friends and family members had affectionately adopted a coding system describing my appetite. Code Green implied a general discomfort but tolerable level of hunger, while Code Yellow was indicative of a half-hour warning that disfunction was near, and finally Code Red was indicative of system shutdown; can't think straight, slurring words, numbness in the hands and other extremities. In contemporary cycling terms, this is known as "bonking". I was in need of calories and carbohydrates of any type and, fortunately, Fredericksburg delivered.

Entering Fredericksburg was a bit like stepping back in time 75 years. The local gas station had been converted into a drive-thru restaurant and was waiting for me to refuel. After a quick purchase of doughnuts, OJ, and an apple, I started to devour my calorie-rich breakfast. Halfway through my grazing, I was interrupted by Lisa, a talkative senior with one of those undeniable personalities who interjected herself into my mealtime. "Well, you missed the crowds we had here two weeks back", she blurted. Without my asking her to elaborate, she continued, saying that the GOBA bike ride had come through town two weeks prior.

Having completed the GOBA in past years with my son, I knew she was referring to the Great Ohio Bike Adventure. This is an event in which some 3,000 bike-riders trek through a 300 to 400-mile course that wind its way through a selected quadrant of the state. The riders swarm into town, each consuming hundreds of calories in a single sitting. It's a great economic boost for any volunteer group or small restaurant that is fortunate enough to be on the GOBA route. Lisa, a former restaurant owner, was not shy about initiating conversation with me. She was also certainly not shy about making known her opinion of the local Amish, either. She liked them and informed me that there are three levels of Amish; high, medium, and low, and each interacts with the public in different ways.

As we continued our conversation, I realized that Lisa's comments revealed a much more insightful respect for the Amish. As an elderly, white-bearded man with a traditional straw hat walked by, Lisa interrupted herself in mid-sentence and blurted, "Hey Frank, how's it going?" The Amish gentleman waved his coffee mug as if to salute and returned the greeting, never intending to disrupt our conversation. I later found that Holmes County contains the highest population of Amish in the country and likely the world, estimated at 36,000. Their common language is a combination of Pennsylvania Dutch and German. Perhaps this explains why the kids back at the bump and dent store were apparently speechless when I entered. And here, I thought it was my bike garb.

With a whole lot more biking ahead and my bladder about to burst from all the coffee talk, I was looking for an easy conversation change. Although probably not the best choice of topic changes, I was curious about her earlier observations and the three levels of Amish. Like many religious groups, there is a majority who are active participants following their creed. There is also a devout branch adhering to the tenants of simple work and placement on earth to serve God's interests. Then there are those who take a more casual view of God's purpose and assume a more practical approach to automation when work is required. Now sweating and in pain of another type I had to excuse myself and find the bathroom quickly. Without much more than a handshake, Lisa and I parted and I ran to the bathroom in the restaurant.

I like to think that we each left with a memory and perspective that we did not have before our meeting. In this instance, I think I received the larger portion of wisdom from this elder Ohioan which made me realize for a moment the benefit of bicycle travel as it creates an opportunity to have a casual conversation without pretense. Moments later and getting back on the road after an interesting conversation, it usually takes a few minutes for me to find my pedal groove and start spinning again. After a few light turns of the pedals (or chain ring for the experienced cyclist) and heading out of Fredericksburg, the road quickly turned into a co-use road, shared between an uncommon pairing of pedestrians and Amish horse buggies. Car traffic was absent on this full-width road. Yellow diamond signs with a black silhouette of a horse carriage were positioned along the road as it passed through an expansive wetland. The traffic of any type was sparse with an occasional Amish carriage and a few cyclists. When approaching each carriage coming in the opposite direction I attempted to make eye contact and a friendly salutation or waving gesture. In each case I received a similar and subtle response from the driver and occasionally the children. Each in an odd way, their waive was quietly distant and a cautionary slow-motion reaction, as if they were on a distant ship. For all I knew maybe we were on two different ships and having a New York State upbringing, maybe I was just being a little too critical.

A few miles later I came up behind three older gentlemen on bikes all traveling at a casual pace together. One was portly and overweight who introduced himself as Joe. Frank was the proud leader of the trio at age 86 and the third an Amish man named Ben. Ben, who had all the traditional trimmings of his upbringing and culture, had a long white beard, a straw hat, work boots, dungarees and yes, I looked, no back pockets. Each were riding new bikes which I found surprising for Ben as I assumed he was more of a traditionalist who did not engage with automation or playtime. As the conversation ensued over the next half hour I was educated on Joe's recent heart attack, and Frank's insistence for Joe to buy a bike and start exercising himself back to health. Ben, the quietest of the bunch was very comfortable riding alongside his partners with his Trek bike and dungarees. Though Ben spoke little I gathered the three were mutual friends and simply out for some fresh air and exercise. Frank was the oldest of all and probably the liveliest, explaining "Once a week we are riding ten miles at a time on this trail". Ben chimed in, "and we will eventually complete the entire trail". Joe then added, "We drove forty miles this morning from Tuscarawas County just to ride, drink our coffee and get back to the car again". "Before Joe has another heart attack" Frank chided! As we headed towards Millersburg I got that strange sense that I had been inserted in a long conversation these old men had been having since boyhood. These were longtime friends that had been riding bikes for years together and could tease each other about life and death, religion, politics and any other subject that caught their fancy. After five miles of friendly banter Frank called out the intersection for their coffee spot and the three departed from the trail. As quickly as we had met, the serendipity of the past half-hour conversation left me with the feeling that Amish Ben was not that different from the rest of us. Though he dressed a little unconventionally for a comfortable bike ride he was equally wise to his surroundings as his partner-riders were.

Back on my own again I noticed on both sides of the road, a vast plain of jade colored lily pads with white blossoms floated on the water's surface. Occasionally, my eye was caught by proverbial bumps on a log, box turtles sitting side-by-side while soaking in the afternoon sun. The steady croaking of frogs created a natural symphony that was the perfect accompaniment to the serene setting of the marsh. I greatly enjoyed traversing the flat miles as nature's bounty unfolded. Below the surface of this vast marsh was an ecosystem with hundreds of native plant and animal species actively engaged in an intertwined spiral of co-existence. Though the surface was calm, there was a certain subtle energy given off. It may have been the bubbles from beneath the beaver dam that appeared on the surface of the marsh. Maybe it was the birds of prey perched on a high limb or the careful stepping of the Blue Heron along the banks of the marsh. Whatever it was, there was a sense that something was about to happen, if only I was patient enough to stop, listen, and observe. As the marsh gradually gave way to a more wooded terrain, the canopy of trees again protected the ground from the sun's penetrating rays. It was clear that this portion of the raised bike path was created through the sweat equity of the canal diggers of years back and which eventually yielded to the trainline.

As I approach each town along the OTET there comes a natural curiosity to see what makes the town tick and what brought it to this spot on the map. With many of Ohio's small populations a rich agricultural capability was necessary to thrive. Later the advances in transportation enabled their product to reach further consumers. A full assortment of circumstantial questions entertains my mind as human history, natural resources, and economic development are all intertwined as a puzzle piece wanting to become part of the bigger picture. A towns growth and survival in the larger spectrum of economy are many times determined by external forces such as urban sprawl or a new and nearby industry, each bringing people and ideas together. Fortunately, the town of Millersburg is experiencing renewed growth from its humble beginnings along the Killbuck Creek as a flower mill. The village now the County Seat for Holmes County boasts a new hotel and other accoutrements of city life. Even the local Walmart boasts a fourteen-bay carriage house for its Amish cliental. Today, the Millersburg train depot conveniently located on the path remains a vestige of historic agriculture and transportation. However, lying beyond train depot and a shallow group of trees sits an active village equipped with a variety of supplies, lodging and food options. I took some time to walk through the repurposed depot now a museum which depicts the once thriving history of Millersburg, Ohio. On other occasion I have found the city to be quite lively with numerous opportunities for dinner in town and a conveniently placed hotel and grocery store just off the trail.

Getting back on my bike and a six-mile ride from Millersburg I came across a dilapidated train depot announcing the town of Killbuck. The old wooden depot painted in faded yellow, showed years of disrepair and overgrowth. I snapped a picture of the town sign thinking there were many more depots to come, with each having a story behind it. Back in the day when travel moved at a slower pace through the Ohio woodlands, the depots were the first sign for the traveler that civilization was approaching. Killbuck, and so many other small towns along the line prospered by the canal and later by the trains. Reading the sign by the Killbuck Depot provided an explanation of the town and its namesake. The Killbuck name came from an Indian Chief of the Delaware Tribe, who supported the formation of our nation's early territorial disputes in the late 1700's.

As the bike path continued further south, small villages like Killbuck, nestled in the rolling hills, reminded me of similar towns and country roads I had traveled through in West Virginia. It also brought to mind a famous song written by John Denver, "Take Me Home, Country Roads". I recognized a comforting sense of transparency with open screen doors, curtains blowing in the midday breeze, and a friendly level of pedestrian traffic on the main street. Riding through town, I spied an older gentleman dressed up which reminded me of a rhinestone cowboy, complete with belt buckle, a turquoise bolo tie, and an old pickup truck nearby. I was surprised to see that he was holding the attention of a group of youngsters outside of a small grocery store. Some were seated on their bikes, some on the tabletop and even more sitting on the bench seat. I was curious and intrigued as to how this unlikely group came about. Meanwhile, my stomach was gurgling again so I decided to park my bike against a railing adjacent to the picnic tables and this gathering of youngsters. The little roadside store did not have much of a selection, so I hastily chose a burger and a Gatorade. I was eager to get back outside to eavesdrop on the conversation. As I listened in, I was not surprised to learn that the nattily dressed gentleman had once been a schoolteacher. The old-timer was engaging each of the kids by name and covering everything from their favorite football teams to computer apps.

At one point, a little girl asked what kind of bike I was riding. I explained that it takes me on long trips and that all my gear is contained in the saddlebags bags in the back. The older gentleman was equally curious about my arrival to Killbuck and asked about my starting point. He was a lifetime resident of the town and appeared to find enjoyment in reaching across multiple generations and learning the simple pleasures of a youngster just released from school for the summer. It seemed as if the retired schoolteacher and the curious children enjoyed the companionship of one another. Before I had finished my lunch, a pair of female riders pulled into town from Route 520. They were on day five of a trip from Cincinnati and explained that in my near future as I was headed southeast the hills were about to return. In particular, they informed me that the immediate climb out of Killbuck on Route 62 was a doozy. As they described the hills, a pit in my stomach was forming. Had I possibly miscalculated my days of travel from Cleveland to Cincinnati? Were the forthcoming hills more than I anticipated? Was I now looking at five to six days? Nonetheless, the challenge called and I pedaled on out of town looking for the Route 62 climb. As the main street took a few turns out of Killbuck, I found my inside voice humming an old Glen Campbell tune, "Rhinestone Cowboy". It wasn't long before I was staring up at the hill the two riders in town had forecast in my future. I quickly slid my hands down on the shift levers of the bike, switching into the granny gear, the smallest gear associated with the pedals of my bike, to ensure a successful climb up this monstrous hill. I was determined to pedal my way up and, at numerous times, had to raise my upper body from the saddle to jog on the pedals to maintain my uphill momentum. After a good effort and a moderate case of oxygen debt, I found myself cheating a glance back down the monster hill as a reward for the effort. I was soon to learn that there were many more hills yet to come.

On one such hill, I saw a large, human-like figure standing alongside the road as it slowly came into view. The silhouette provided few details but it carried a rather odd hunch to its posture. As I continued past this motionless figure and on through the open and rolling hills of the Ohio pasturelands, I realized that I had just crossed paths with the mystical Bigfoot. Right here in Holmes County, Ohio. No kidding! A life-sized, 10-foot, concrete Bigfoot statue was poised outside a fabrication factory on this old country road. Sure enough, around the corner were a dozen or more baby (smaller) Bigfoot statues. I couldn't help but laugh at the poor guy who brings home one of these lawn ornaments, "Hey Honey, look what I found!" At best, maybe a statue of Bigfoot could be used as a good college dorm prank.

After subsequent visits to the Holmes County trail a series of OTET improvements have resulted in a re-routing around the "killer hill" in Killbuck. For the time being the Route 520 takes riders out of Killbuck and into the town of Glenmont, eight miles later. Talking with the director of trails in Holmes County the path will ultimately connect Killbuck to Glenmont with a bike path segment which avoids the heavily traveled Route 520 and the killer hill in Killbuck. I also understand their plans include a primitive campsite for those hardier travelers carrying their own gear and needing a short overnight respite.

Standing tall in the middle of Glenmont village boasts an old sand stone church that was constructed from locally quarried materials. Just down the road on Route 520 is the Briar Hill Stone Company which has been extracting sand stone since the turn of the century. The Quarry has been the source of a unique grade of colored sandstone used for numerous structures such as the Dayton Art Museum, monuments in Washington DC and numerous local churches. Recalling the new Pavilion in Edgewater Park, I learned that it was also faced with sand stone from this quarry. Looking through the show room, the samples hanging on the wall show a wide range of red and brown hues which make for an attractive option when building.

Some of the newest additions to the OTET are occurring in the Glenmont area along the Holmes County Trail. With challenging inclines still in the area, the difficult roads and street traffic are replaced with some of Ohio's beautiful unspoiled hardwood forests. Getting lost in the wooded scenery, a long incline soon reverses its slope and becomes a favorable downhill into the Mohican Valley Trail.

Even with the hills of the Holmes County Trail behind me, I could still feel the resultant burning pain in my legs. Remembering Road Rule Number Four, (*For every hill there is an equal and opposite hill*), the southbound trail provided a nice payback in the form of an easy descent into the Mohican Valley Trail. Along the way, signs for the state's "Longest Covered Bridge", aka The Bridge of Dreams, was seen. As the path continues across the 200-meter bridge, clearly designated for pedestrian traffic only. I was amazed to see a couple on a three-wheeled motorcycle–commonly referred to as a trike–with a trailer in tow, trying numerous times to ride their vehicle across the bridge. Each attempt they made resulted in them getting pinched off by the narrowness of the bridge walls as they battled with the girth of their vehicle. Another couple and I watched as the riders finally came to the conclusion that this was not a good idea. It was a classic case of one's eyes being too big for the stomach. The trike couple finally gave up and turned their vehicle around to exit the park in the same direction from which they had come. Once the bridge was cleared, the pedestrian traffic was able to enjoy the converted train track high above the streambed.

As the day drifted along, I discovered that a number of train depots had been converted to convenient rest stations for pedestrian and bike traffic. From a historical perspective, these were the connection points for numerous towns that developed into economic centers for commerce and human transport across Ohio. After a short, 30-year lifespan, the locomotive largely replaced the Erie Canal system. Over time, the complications of flooding and low water levels proved the locomotive to be a more reliable form of transportation. Combined with the carrying capacity and speed benefits of rail, the Ohio legislators began to redirect funding in support of the train before the canals were completely developed. Whether by train or by boat, the names of destinations such as Killbuck, Danville, Mount Vernon, Sunbury, Gambier, Westerville, and Columbus became intersecting points of trade and commerce. In many locations along the trail, the side-by-side legacy of each mode of transportation had given way to the bike path. With your eyes closed and the assistance of a gentle breeze, you just may hear the sound of the conductor calling out these town names that will forever echo in the woods as you pedal from point to point.

As the Mohican Valley Trail merges into the Kokosing Gap Trail further to the west, a particularly beautiful section of mature Ohio woodland awaits the rider west of Kenyan College and Gambier Township. The bike trail takes advantage of the now-retired rail system and has numerous overhead bridge structures standing as out-of-place in the forest as monoliths, representative of a time long since its prime. I pulled into Mount Vernon in the mid afternoon and decided to grab dinner at a restaurant where I hoped to plug in my electronic gadgets. My new cell phone had not been tested and was already out of juice. Of course, this is a slap in the face of Road Rule Number Six.

Road Rule Number Six
Let go of the electronics, use your surroundings, and use your senses.

"Baby, be a simple, really simple man. Oh, be something you love and understand." Lynyrd Skynyrd, Simple Man

This is not about the resistance to using electronics or popular GPS and experience-enhancing tools. It is about raising your awareness to your experiences. As our technology gets better and better, it also insulates us from our immediate surroundings. It hides in plain sight and can make us oblivious to danger. If you're staring at your GPS, you're losing out not only on the immediate scenery but also may be unaware of that pothole in the road just 10 feet in front of you. Put the watch away. Watches are used for keeping appointments. Some of the best days on the road have a start and end point with the rising and setting of the sun. Allow the entire course of the day to be a series of random and unexpected events.

The last time I checked, your body will tell you when to eat, sleep, and relieve yourself. It's okay to find a park during a midday ride, pull up under a broad-leafed oak to take shelter from the mid-afternoon sun, and just take a nap. You're on autopilot now. You may just find that the slice of freedom from your highly structured and complex "other life" is what you have been craving for years.

In case you were wondering, I used to be old school; maps and compass all the way. However, with the usefulness of GPS units as well as safety issues that are often addressed using these devices, navigating areas with sometimes interchangeable street names and confusing route numbers can be less complicated than the old school way of having to refer to old, outdated maps and route numbers for guidance and direction. In the name of full disclosure, it is quite likely that I will include a GPS unit in my gear on my next cycling adventure.

Road Rule Number Six, talks about using your surroundings and your senses. While usually a very good rule to follow, on this ride -and with executive authority–I decided to modify this rule in the event of an emergency. With my wife's parting words, "Don't forget to call", in mind, this was all the reason I needed for the modification.

A hot and dusty wind blowing across the outlying Mount Vernon streets gave the town the feel of the classic Clint Eastwood spaghetti western, *The Good the Bad and the Ugly*, with the familiar flute piece repeating itself. All that was needed to complete the Western drama was for tumbleweed to blow across my path. Circling around the city block a couple times, I decided to eat dinner at a local pizza shop. I was hot, salty, and parched and consequently was escorted to a corner table away from the other guests. Once seated, I proceeded to spread out my maps and plug in my electronic toys. With a cold pitcher of lemonade on the table sweating with condensation and a pizza on the way, the evening was starting to feel complete. After dinner I rode a short distance to work off the heavy carb rich dinner I just consumed. Shortly thereafter my attention was captured as an iconic Train Depot sign announcing Mount Vernon was formidably hanging from the buildings large eves. Dismounting the bike for a quick photo, the depot was in much better shape than the last one I passed in Killbuck and was recently restored with a restroom inside. Now, the depot is a great source for visitor information, placed right alongside the bike path. Afterwards I took a walk through the Mount Vernon city streets and found the normal buzz of pedestrians and local traffic within the sleepy town. An active restoration of the Woodward Playhouse, purportedly the oldest free-standing structure of its kind was in progress. And the Mount Vernon Grand Hotel sitting prominently on the corner of the town square, is a place worth a second look or a possible stay if you're looking for a posher overnight excursion. Extending my break, a little bit longer I stopped at a trendy coffee shop for a caffeine fix. The underlying college ethos, had groups of students engaged in team discussion on an upcoming project. All of this left me with the sense that the city was making a resurgence as the downtown continues to rehabilitate.

After my relaxing coffee break pedaling back to the train depot, I was back off the bike again to visit the reclaimed glass foundry also known as the Pittsburg Plate Glass Company No. II, or PPG. Similar to the other renovation projects in the center of Mount Vernon the first evidence of this park's reclamation effort is a 280-foot smoke stack with a staircase spiraling upwards around the outside of the tower. What is also known as Ariel Foundation Park, is an interesting place just to wander as the old glass works property, has now been transformed into a 240-acre walking park and a place for a variety of entertainment. With old quarries converted to fishing lakes and architectural remnants scattered about, the artful displays of this turn of the century industry hide the fact that it once boasted to be the largest plate glass factory in the world. Look for the large chunks of aqua colored glass sparkling in the sun as a reminder of this once booming industry. And, if your so inclined take a hike up the spiral stare case it provides a spectacular view of Mount Vernon and of the Kokosing River below.

Heading out of the Mount Vernon area, I started to look for a quiet spot to set up my tent. The summer solstice in Ohio now pushed the sunset back to nearly 9:00pm on Ohio's western border. Before long with a relaxing pace, I found myself with a few miles of post-dinner riding and in the middle of acres of wistful wheat waving in the breeze. Finally, the coming darkness encouraged me to set up camp. Once settled in, I started putting pencil to paper as the sun cast its long shadows over the rolling field.

Unfortunately, the peaceful evening was short-lived as dusk turned to darkness and darkness to pre-dawn, the return of the dreaded snorting blasts from an upset deer became the early morning's intonation... again. A couple of glances through the tent screening revealed nothing but an unusually cool night with a full moon casting a glaze over a fog-covered field. With a second disrupted night's sleep, I was feeling unusually punchy. This led me to the humorous explanation that the same buck from the night before had been following me for the past 80 miles along the bike path and was here to haunt me again. This time, I muffled my ears with some loose clothing and fought for a few more moments of sleep.

Edgewater Park
Cleveland

Ceremonial Start in Lake Erie
Edgewater Park
Cleveland

Cuyahoga Valley Scenic
Railroad
Peninsula

Lock Four, Cuyahoga River Valley
Canal Fulton

Tunneling through
Cuyahoga Valley
National Park
Peninsula

Lilly Pads
Summit Lake Akron

Long Boat Crew
Canal Fulton

Bridge of Dreams
Brinkhaven

Multi-purpose road sign
Millersburg

Areal Foundation Tower
Mount Vernon

Cross Country Travelers along the OTET
Millersburg

Geographic Center of Ohio
Centerburg

Alum Creek Bridge
Columbus

Scioto River
Columbus

State Bike Route 1

Stealth Camping along the Bike Path

Daniel Boone's Knife
Greene County Historical Society

Wright Brothers Memorial
Miami Valley Trail System (connector trail from Xenia to Dayton)

Butterworth Station
Underground railroad site
Warren County

Traveler Sign-in Board
Loveland

John A. Roebling Bridge
Cincinnati

Queen City Sign
Cincinnati

Day Three
Mount Vernon to South Charleston - 105 miles

After another disruptive night's sleep, I realized that the unseasonably cool evenings and insufficient bedding had me waking up tired and irritable. Clearly, I have should have made the last-minute adjustment and brought my goose-down sleeping bag instead of the fleece bag. Regardless of my restless night, the road was waiting and a dark 6:30am start saw my first rotation of the wheels.

A new headlight for the bike is proving to be the MacGyver tool of the trip as it doubles for evening and morning light assistance, no flashlight necessary. The blackness of the early morning surrounded my passage through the trail and was alleviated with the assistance of my single beam headlight. Slowly, the song of the day eased into my foggy memory; "Up with the sun, gone with the wind. She always said I was lazy". With a quick passing of the morning ride, I pieced together the rest of the words to Bob Seger's "Traveling Man" and hummed the melody to myself.

Traveling towards Centerburg I found the bike path to pass by an open and non-descript grassy park with a gravel driveway. Uninspired to stop I rode by unaware of its content. After a second thought I did notice a large boulder in the middle of the field and a flagpole near its base. Deciding it was worth a second look, I slowly circled around and rode my bike right up to the rather large and out of place boulder that had been used to commemorate the spot. With a quick read of the bronze plaque mounted to the bolder I was surprised to find this to be the geographic center of Ohio. With a quick picture and a reading of the plaque, I smirked at the simplicity of the town's name and its association to the states geographic center.

Looking for a little diversity from the bike trail and from the beaten path I took a southern route off the OTET to pass through an appealing village of Hartford, Ohio. The small village center consists of a green, about an acre in size, with an older town hall building centered on the lawn. An original water pump was still working and served me well to refresh my water bottles. A well-worn city block made of traditional red "paver" bricks with shops and private residences surrounding the green, all gave the ambiance of an old colonial village like those I had seen on my bike travels through rural Connecticut. The tight-knit community around the green had not awoken as I walked around the block. The realization of a fresh breakfast was going to elude me again and I opted for the usual nuts and fruit stored away in one of the pockets of my panniers.

Soon after leaving my colonial New England experience in Ohio, I returned to the trail and rode into the town of Sunbury, an old stagecoach town with its beginnings dating back to the early 1800's. For decades, Sudbury was the intersection of two major routes, the Walhonding Trail and the Delaware Newark Pike. This Midwestern town saw the likes of Presidents', William Henry Harrison, Rutherford Hayes, and local legend Johnny Appleseed. Today, the town boasts the historic Sunbury Inn and numerous other shops and restaurants located around the city block sized green. Located within the municipal green boasts a life-sized wood carving of John Chapman (Johnny Appleseed) with a tin pot for a hat, an ax for pruning and a burlap bag for distributing his apple seeds. Johnny was a local legend throughout the Midwest in the late 1700's and is responsible for many of the areas numerous apple orchards.

For my immediate fuel needs, an old-fashioned 1950's era doughnut shop served as a perfect stopping point to grab breakfast. While savoring my second cup of java, I took stock of my body ailments and noticed that my knees were a bit achy. However, I was pleasantly surprised to note that my hips had not been aggravated by all the activity. It's a common joke amongst my running friends that my 50,000-mile warranty had been exceeded following a 35-year running career. So far, the bike is allowing me to get an extended rider on the policy. Aches and pains aside, Sunbury is another town worth revisiting to absorb the local history and staying at the old Sunbury Inn looks like a possible weekend bucket list activity.

Leaving Sunbury and traveling down Old 3C Highway a short distance, I came to the small town of Galena where my map and compass skills were again challenged. A poorly placed sign on the road suggested a false left-hand turn onto the bike path that resulted in a five-mile departure from my intended route. Unfortunately, this detour included some significant hill work from which I would have to recover at a later time. Luckily, a fellow cyclist helped me regain my bearings and find my way back to Galena. Being familiar with the route, he mentioned that his local bike club was trying to improve the signage, allowing "touring bikers" easier passage. Having returned to Galina a number of times since the original trip, I found the markings much clearer. If you're looking for more food options the small main street; also known as the Old 3C Highway serves as the towns primary intersection and access to a couple of nice dining options. If you choose to stay on the OTET path, you may want to take a look at the historic Hoover Mud Flats and boardwalk from which the origin of the Galena Brick Company was created at the turn of the 19th century. Today, a stroll through the town finds some of the houses that were built using these locally produced materials. On return visits to Galina, local cyclists have gone out of their way to ensure travelers are heading in their intended direction, always happy to share their town's history.

As the day progressed, the bike path continued to weave carefully in parallel with the Old 3C Highway, an old transportation artery to Columbus. The scenery started to change from reservoir park to urban life. Also gone were the challenging rural hills of Holmes County which subtly changes to a beautifully manicured, white pine encased stretch along the Hoover Reservoir for about ten miles. A trailside fire station usually provides a convenient water stop for those needing a bottle refill.

Entering the northwest corner of Columbus through Westerville and Dublin the scenery gradually evolves from suburban housing, to urban commercial businesses, and comes with an increase in traffic. Soon the trailhead for the Alum Creek Trail, becomes visibly and artfully crosses over the creek and nearby streets with a series of beautifully designed bridges. Each in its own right a study in architecture and an immersion in its natural surroundings. Laminated wood arches, black iron structures, steel cross ties, wooden planking, concrete and stone abutments are carefully integrated in the park as an homage to the old artisan craftmanship that the surrounding city was built upon. While enjoying the winding bends and turns of the Alum Creek Trail I stopped at a historic marker to read its contents. The marker served as a somber reminder of the river's use as part of the Underground Railroad. The 58 miles of Alum Creek running predominantly north to south served as the "Liquid Lines of Freedom" for runaway slaves escaping a life of bondage and brutality. During the evening hours, freedom seekers waded through the Alum Creek in an effort to evade both bloodhound and Bounty hunters. Several homes along nearby Sunbury Road were used as "stations" for the northern passage to freedom. Alum Creek and numerous other waterways and tributaries were strung together creating a corridor of protection as they reached the shores of Lake Erie and ultimately Canada.

Despite regaining my sense of awareness for city traffic, numerous street changes made for tedious mapping. At an awkwardly large intersection I came across a senior, on the opposite side of the street. She was nervously waiting for the signal to change so she could make her crossing. Seeing her despair I leaned my bike against the light pole and crossed the intersection. Erma was local to Dublin and was on her way to the grocery store with her two-wheel cart. Out of general curiosity for each other, we struck up a warm conversation at this busy intersection. She was a 76-year-old widow who wore a pair of oversized framed glasses. Comically, her eyes appeared much larger than normal. She had been enduring macular degeneration in both eyes for the past 10 years but her energy and enthusiasm for life gave me the impression that she was a teenager with a pass to skip school for the day. As she began asking about my trip it became comical to me that she only had one temple on her glasses. Because of this, her glasses kept slipping down her face as we talked. I interrupted our discussion midstream to show her that I was perplexed with the same problem, as I had been sporting around with the same one-armed condition on my 2.0 readers. Together, we laughed at our situation and how silly we looked as well as the fact that we were determined to live with the condition rather than buy replacement glasses. As we talked, it was obvious that Erma needed to get on with her chores for the day. Being an old Eagle Scout, I offered to take her across the street. She graciously accepted and I escorted her across. We exchanged best wishes on the other side of the street and, with that, we were each back on our way.

This exchange between total strangers has recurred numerous times throughout my travels and serves as a reminder that people are genuinely approachable and that the circumstances of life bring open participants together in the most unlikely times and places. This exchange with Erma and the many others will remain with me as fond memories through the years. Soon afterwards I arrived at the Westerville Train Depot that was equipped with restroom, water refill and a mini bike station for most moderate adjustments that your bike may need.

Road Rule Number Seven
Riding alone doesn't mean
you're lonesome.

Fellow cyclist Bob Howells once wrote, "When you travel as a group, you're viewed as a group. You're assumed to be collectively self-sufficient. When you're alone, others see you as a fellow human being. People readily share their humanity with you. The earth and the people within unfold in proportion to your openness to them. Each of us has travel preferences that may include solo riding, group riding, or even event riding. The solo option in cycling opens the door to new acquaintances that may change your way of thinking." Road Rule Number Seven is not so much about riding alone as it is about knowing what you want from a ride and how to best achieve these desires. The seasoned traveler may be in search of a new destination such as an unexplored national park. The young adventurer may want to navigate across a trail with GPS and the athlete may want to pound out mega miles; like a hundred miles day. In the end, there is a personal reward for each type of cyclist whether in large groups or as a soloist. Determine your motivations for riding; pick the options that best suit your desired travel, and ride with purpose. The long miles in the saddle will teach you to appreciate your surroundings with all of your senses and challenge you to look into your soul.

Entering downtown Columbus from the North requires a watchful eye as numerous intersecting bike paths cross the OTET. Please refer to the Columbus Trail Maps provided in the Appendix to add clarity to your travels. For the next two miles, starting with the overpass of Morse Road, the Alum Creek Trail changes to the Columbus Downtown Connector and then ends with the intersection of Jack Gibbs Boulevard and Cleveland Avenue. With a series of South easterly turns on city streets the well-marked OTET will navigate the rider towards the Scioto River and Greenway. The bike path picks up again at the intersection of W. Long Street and Neil Avenue. This is one of the rare sections of the OTET where the independently developed trails do not conveniently connect with each other. City planners are continuing to close this short mile and a half separation between these two terminuses and we will live with this inconvenience for a few more years until funding and resources are appropriated. Though the bike path is replaced with city street, there is a healthy sidewalk through most of this section allowing the rider to travel safely. As with any city travel I am cautious to avoid rush hour traffic, and generally turn on my blinking head and taillights for added visibility and safety. During this short city section, a popular chain hotel and some nearby food options are conveniently located if this happens to be an end point for your day.

During my 2014 travels the OTET took me through a difficult mapping exercise now remembered fondly as the Olentangy quagmire. A combination of poor city street signage, inadequate park maps and numerous tangent trails left this rider very much confused. The park itself was beautiful but my sense of direction and navigating from one end of the park to the other was turned inside out. Today the OTET trail has been rerouted to avoid the Olentangy area and is replaced with the Alum Creek Trail, allowing for an easier entry into Columbus, the states capitol. The Olentangy "experience" did however remind me of another Road Rule.

Road Rule Number Eight

Know where you are and where you want to be. When in doubt, use multiple maps including state, local or trail.

The obvious reaction to this road rule is to employ the use of a GPS unit. However, many have experienced regions where even the best electronic devices lose reception or experience a blackout. Whether the GPS is your primary or secondary tool for navigation, it is important to know your bearings and to know that you're maintaining the planned trajectory or direction. Learn about the areas through which you will be traveling. Use natural features in your surroundings to keep your bearings correct.

While on a bicycle and generally in congested or urban environments, the need for confirming location checks increases when compared to the speed of a backpacker. There will be numerous challenges for the cyclists attempting to navigate through the congestion of information and traffic. Common mistakes on the cycling road include missed turns, hidden street signs, route numbers for road names, detours, and even good intentions but wrong directions. Each of these challenges can have a potentially disastrous effect.

Many years ago in rural Faulkton, South Dakota, I took a turn on an old county road, thinking that I could avoid a strong east-

erly head wind and later return to my east heading when the wind died down. Though the Triple AAA state maps showed my location and where I ultimately wanted to be, it certainly did not show the conditions I was about to experience along the way. What started as a formal asphalt road deteriorated progressively to the condition of a trail and I soon found myself in a fool's bet. Each reduction in road quality was met with the optimism that this was a temporary degradation and that the traveling surface would surely return to asphalt in the next mile. Twenty miles later, my wheels sinking in loose soil and surrounded by corn stalks, I was barely able to see the rooftop of the next farmhouse. Having made a decision to cut my losses, I found a farmer who admired my effort to visit him and he redirected me back down the road I had just traveled. I did return to town in time for lunch after a 40 mile mistake, a much humbled and wiser rider.

So the point of this Road Rule is to use all of the available resources–maps, local people, and GPS. Keep yourself informed to the largest extent possible as to where you are and where you want to be.

Regardless of the environment, it is easy to get turned around without perspective. For those without elaborate GPS-equipped bikes (like mine), the challenge is to maintain a bird's eye view with a state map for a general heading. Comparing that state map with a city map or a local street-level map for details and possible directional cues. Even with these maps in hand, the city streets in and around Columbus made me feel like a mouse in a maze. A wise scoutmaster once told me that when you're lost–in the woods, in the city, and metaphorically in life–it is most important to "know where you are and where you want to be". These are the first steps to recovery and have always served as good advice.

For those intent on camping their way through Ohio, I advise not attempting to camp in the Columbus Camp Chase Trail area as this is a heavily populated area. Through riders heading south on the OTET are best advised to travel beyond Battelle Darby

Creek Metro Park. I was happy to return back to the bike path and experience some of the other historical gems in the area. Soon I approached the Camp Chase Trail portion of the OTET. With a name that sounded like a tribute to an old war hero I pulled over and curiously googled Camp Chase to see what historical significance this area held. Now a Nationally Registered Historic Place, Camp Chase was originally established in 1861 as a military training camp called Camp Jackson. Later it was changed to Camp Chase and used as a Confederate prison camp during the American Civil War. This was not a pleasant place to be and at one time housed over 8,000 men with limited rations and poor sanitation, many did not survive. Today, the park includes over 2,200 Confederate grave sites and is a grim reminder of the lives lost while in captivity.

As the bike path crosses Sullivant Avenue the park unfolds for the rider and can be explored by those with a greater interest of the Civil War era. The Camp Chase Trail follows alongside an active railroad line as it takes riders out of Columbus proper and into the nearby suburbs and communities. There are a number of street crossings that continue to remind the rider that your still very much in an active city requiring careful attention. Be sure to look for the side of the Pittsburg Plate Glass industrial building that has the entire back side painted with a silhouette mural of the entire OTET experience! The informative mural provides mileage distances showing that your 144 miles from Cleveland and 107 miles from Cincinnati, depending on your chosen direction. The mural also displays the silhouettes of the three major cities of Ohio that the OTET traverses; Cleveland, Columbus and Cincinnati.

Exiting Columbus, the trail resumes to flat suburban travel with an occasional expanse of farmland over the next five miles. Before long, Battelle Darby Creek Metro Park becomes a notable point of interest as the OTET swings through the park and down to the creek on a short gravel path. The park is notable for its confluence of the Big Darby Creek and the Little Darby Creek. The park also has significance of a scientific nature as it boasts a riparian ecosystem that includes over 140 fresh water species of fish and mollusks. In all candor I had to google riparian to find its meaning to be the ecosystem where river meets land. Today, the wonderfully diverse park is enjoyed by many, young and old. Enjoying the changing scenery and the diverse history outside of Columbus made me lose track of time and to some degree the many miles of path I had yet to complete. The mid-afternoon sun bearing down on the path and the radiant heat was noticeable but not unbearable. Looking at my trail maps I knew I had a long 11-mile section with minimal cross roads and traffic interruption until reaching the next town of London. If there is ever a place to make up lost time on the OTET this is where the opportunistic cyclists can find advantage. Positioning my hands in the lower handlebar drops with my head down to avoid the wind, I built up a head of steam that resulted in an 18-mile-an-hour pace, that I was fortunately enough to continue for the next ten miles. Occasionally, I looked up only to find large expanses of land making up the heartland of Ohio.

Since my original travels down the OTET, I was pleasantly surprised to find a number of community service, Eagle Scout projects outside London. Each providing a lean-to styled shelter for picnicking or possibly an emergency shelter. Riding further through the town of London, I noticed a carefully crafted wrought iron sign spelling out in large three-foot-high red-letters, LONDON which identified entry into town with certainty. It also identifies a small park that is dedicated as a sanctioned "primitive campground" for those seeking a quick overnight camp and is reasonably secluded from road traffic. A set of eight foot by eight-foot platforms with common decking material serves a raised bed to place a tent on and avoid most moisture and bug concerns. Reading a posting on a nearby information board by the picnic shelter provided directions to public restroom and potable water. All of this is carefully reserved for those traveling the trail and prepared for a more primitive overnight arrangement. Since my original travels in 2014, there has been a significant increase and interest for primitive overnight travel along the OTET. As the trail continues to grow in popularity so too will the flow of traffic from the cycle touring community. The OTET Fund continues to work with local municipalities to strike the right balance and service for this growing brand of travel.

Recently I met an energetic young couple on the OTET, who were riding their bikes across the country from Portland, Oregon to Portland, Maine. Katie and Jeff were each independently self-sustained; carrying their camping gear, utilitarian supplies, and rations of food. They were truly excited to find London's trail side accommodations as it took any guesswork out of setting up camp along the trail. This brand of light weight travel is known for a "Leave No Trace Behind" discipline of travel. As we talked, their goals are to simply travel the country side and experience diversity of our nations rich history and bring home memories and photos of their experience. Katie and Jeff did complete their trip of over 5,000 miles and have been sharing their experience with many others. Located in the Appendix are the basic tenants and code of conduct this hardy brand of travelers aspires to achieve.

The trail to South Charleston is another ten miles of wide open farmland that can challenge the most disciplined rider. Long miles of flat trail surrounded by endless horizons of rolling hills of tilled soil or a bountiful sea of corn can test the senses of even a resilient rider. Encouragingly from the sea of corn fields a sign for South Charleston appears on the trail and the bike path turns seamlessly into local suburban streets. I was ready to put down stakes just about anywhere in town after an emotionally exhausting day. Just as my thoughts about the day's ride were winding down, I rode past the charming Houstonia Bed and Breakfast. I thought this would be a nice change of pace after sleeping poorly under the stars for the past couple of nights. If nothing else, at least a backyard spot with a garden hose would suffice and improve my overall disposition. Without a preplanned reservation I suspected my chances of getting a last-minute opening were slim. A doubtful knock on the door, and a silent response simply confirmed my expectation, and so to any thought of a clean and restful night's sleep.

Collecting myself after this false hope, I returned to the bike and noticed the speedometer was showing 95 miles for the day. Staring back at the 95 miles made me feel as if the speedometer was taunting me to break the century mark of 100 miles for the day. The term "century" is a cyclist's shorthand reference for a good day's cycling effort. The century rider gets the same sort of satisfaction from the completion of this effort as a marathoner does in crossing the finish line at the end of a 26.2 mile run. Achieving this distance is uncommon, especially while carrying an additional load of supplies. Somewhere in this day, I was going to hit 100 miles even if it meant circling around town a couple of times.

Before heading out of town I decided to take a break at a local pizzeria for rest and refuel. Downing the delicious carbohydrates had an effect similar to jet fuel for this engine of motion. A large pizza and a couple of lemonade drinks later, I felt rejuvenated to the point of pursuing a few more miles and achieving that elusive century mark. Before picking up my maps and notes in the pizza shop a young staff attendant asked where I was headed. He warned me not to camp too close to Xenia. "You don't want to be there", he said with a tone of authority. Having known the town of Xenia from many years of running races there, I dismissed this as a high school-crosstown rivalry and determined to continue on making my way towards Xenia. Back in the saddle with a belly full of pizza, I returned to the familiar churning of the pedals and headed out of South Charleston. However, before exiting South Charleston there was another point of interest preserved on the outskirts of town that I had to check out. Surrounding the bike path on either side, are a series of carefully restored buildings representing decades of housing along the train line. An 1820's log cabin, a beautifully detailed South Charleston Train Depot and a pair of rail cars from the Pennsylvania Rail Road Line, each nicely restored are amongst other buildings of local historic interest.

A few miles down the path of endless cornfields, I got off my bike and gave a primal victory shout for hitting the 100-mile mark. Of course, other than the birds, no one was in the vicinity to care. I took a celebratory picture of the speedometer as it turned over to 100 miles a big deal for a rider with a loaded bike.

Road Rule Number Nine
Embrace your eccentricity.

Everyone has one.
Your mission is to find out what yours is.

It is truly an enlightening sensation to wake up every day in the outdoors with only one purpose–to find out what the day has in store for you. Some days are packed full of stimulation and others are... well... just plain boring. They could be flat, hot, and lacking companionship or they could be just a long, long grind. To the untrained mind, this can be pure torture and, quite honestly, the reason why endurance sport has a bad rap.

When in a rut, I have found a couple of practices to help break up the tedium of long distance riding. The first practice is something I label as associative thinking. Creating a hyper interest and curiosity in every facet of the ride leads to a more efficient performance but also breaks the monotony. Questions that come to mind include monitoring my cadence, miles, speed, ease of breathing, or the distance to the next grocery store. In the meantime, the miles melt away.

The other technique used is known as dissociative thinking. This requires a little creative courage but is equally effective at curing boredom. Your mind is a wonderful tool that can launch a thousand thoughts and emotions from poetic verse to favorite song lyric or a charming line from a movie. When alone on the long, desolate road, you can conjure any rock star you want to be. Go ahead and belt out a couple of favorite tunes. So what if you're off key or miss a word or two. It's the emotion from deep inside tied with the song that brings a rush of feelings. Though I risk dating myself, you may be surprised what comes from your soul, lying just beneath your boredom–possibly a Bob Seger tune or a line from Monty Python and the Holy Grail. For the intellectuals, it could be reciting the Gettysburg Address. Unless you're a karaoke regular, I recommend making sure there's plenty of space between you and anyone in earshot.

The peddling was surprisingly easier after a crowning century day and a belly full of food. I started looking in earnest for a place to bed down and noticed the orange glint of a flickering flame in the evening dusk. Cautiously, riding closer to glow and past a couple homes along the path a group of revelers were gathered in their reclining chairs huddled around a cinderblock fire pit. The animated group of partygoers appeared to be enjoying each other's company while tending to their fire. A large radio and a family sized cooler of favorite libations was in the shadows near-by likely to keep the party alive and well through the night. Wanting nothing more than to bed down after a long day's ride, I casually passed by with a wave of the hand. Riding by virtually unnoticed the scene gradually came together for me as I noticed, off in the distance a good 200 yards from the bike path, a large, two-bay garage with an awful, gut-wrenching noise coming from within. Clearly, the parents were off at a safe distance from their kids' struggling attempt at forming a grunge rock band. The guttural screaming along with an over-amplified guitarist and drummer was just enough to drive any inhabitant from their home. I was amazed at how far down the path I had to travel before out-distancing the grunge noise. Some half to three -quarters of a mile later, the guitar sound was no longer audible and the thumping beat of the drum was no longer piercing the otherwise calm, midwestern evening. It was time to bed down for the night.

With my tent set-up along the bike path and no one in sight in either direction of the path, I watched the sun set over the ocean of farmland corn. With the sun not entirely settled beyond the horizon, it felt odd to lay down with unused daylight at 9:00 in the evening. With a 105-mile day behind me, and Cincinnati another 80 miles to the southwest, it was conceivable to think I could reach Cincinnati by nightfall the next day. By plan, my son (a second-year student at the University of Cincinnati) was waiting to receive me for a short time. However, as I drifted off to sleep the thought of contacting Sean without a working phone was troubling me. I would need to be creative tomorrow to make a connection.

Day Four
South Charleston to Cincinnati - 95 Miles

While rolling up my damp tent and packing up my overnight gear for the next leg of my trip, I discovered some uninvited stowaway passengers from the night before. It appears that the field in which I slept was a perfect place for garden-variety slugs to be attracted to my body heat. At least a half dozen of the slimy critters were folded, pressed, and dried out from the pressure of my tightly wound tent. Others had surprisingly survived yesterday's long ride. In either case, they are a mess to deal with, sticking to everything outside the tent. Oddly, I also heard a rather vocal clutch of birds quarreling back and forth without a care for my presence. The dense thicket they chose to hide in made it difficult to find the cause of their commotion. My initial guess was the likely offenders were a couple of grouse or possibly our state bird, the cardinal trying to defend its mating territory.

The wheels were rolling by 6:00am with the early morning sunrays on the path indicating another nice day ahead. However, looming in the distance behind me was a familiar red sky glowing through the underbelly of the low, moisture-bearing clouds. The polar vortex had made this trip nearly perfect with temperatures averaging 78 degrees and with little humidity. With an old mariners reference in mind–"red sky in morning, sailors take warning"–the threat of rain appeared imminent.

Predicting my weather fortunes without electronic hardware, I was reminded of Road Rule Number Six; let go of your electronics. Even though I was trying to keep my cellphone charged for reports of my progress back to my wife, I was trying to not otherwise rely on my phone. This meant I had to read the signs provided by Mother Nature which I knew could prepare me for imminent weather challenges and would allow me the opportunity to find cover from severe weather, all without electronics.

The early mornings have been cool and dark requiring warm weather gear to start. My favorite articles of clothing include a winter hat and gloves, my trusty leg warmers (a holdover from my 1983 cross-country trip), tights, baggy bike shorts, and a yellow windbreaker. This unconventional look, uniquely Looney and bordering on Bohemian, was layered in a way that allowed items to be easily stripped off when temperatures start to warm up.

As my body started to warm up to the early morning motion a little melody started to form in my mind. My song of the day came in two parts. First, was the 1978 classic by Kenny Rogers, *"The Gambler"– You got to know when to hold 'em, know when to show 'em*. The second, equally memorable song later became the choice for my morning karaoke with no care for harmony or lyric accuracy. It just felt good to belt out a couple of chords of "You've Lost That Loving Feeling", the 1980 version by Hall and Oates, (no disrespect for the earlier Righteous Brothers version from the '60s). Thankfully, there were no other humans along the path to see or hear this spectacle.

The next five miles on the way to Cedarville were rather uncomfortable as my undercarriage was feeling a bit sensitive, no doubt due to yesterday's 100-miles. A constant shifting in the saddle and a healthy dose of a popular diaper rash cream was required in order to get through the discomfort. However, after another 50 -miles down the road, the memory of distress in this area would mash together anyway.

For the first time in the trip, a coffee shop presented itself at the time of need. This was going to be a good day I thought to myself. Generally, when getting on the road early, breakfast is a handful of nuts, dried fruit, and leftover Gatorade from the day before. God forbid there would be a repeat of that nasty breakfast drink from a couple of days earlier. Entering Cedarville, the morning sun was beaming down on the main street of this small, out-of-session college town. The sun's rays cast their orange glow on the Bean and Cream coffee shop. Was this a dream? All that was missing was angels and harp music. On my first pass at 6:30, the shop appeared closed but I spied one customer inside and decided to make an entry.

Like a scene to any popular western I tied my trusted 85-pound loaded steel donkey to a bike rack out front. Having an unlimited choice of seating in the shop, I selected a window table and purchased a large coffee, muffin, and smoothie, good enough for round one. As the first infusion of caffeine coursed its way through my veins, the subtle warming effect of the coffee prepared me for catching up on my journal notes. Minutes later, a steady stream of people began to pour in and a buzz of the day's activities filled the air.

As I made my second trip to the counter, a burly patron shouted out, "Hey, I haven't seen leg warmers like those in years". The shop went silent waiting for my reaction. I replied proudly that I was the original owner of these 30-year-old, scrunchy leg warmers and I was sure Irene Cara would be happy to sell him her other pair on eBay. Of course, you would have to be a student of the 1980's movie, *Flashdance*, to get the reference. We both laughed at my functional but outdated apparel and we seized the opportunity to talk about how the bike path has brought visitors to Cedarville. We went on for a while before I returned to writing, realizing that I eventually needed to get some miles in before the rain started.

After a hearty breakfast, I got back on the bike and resumed my ride. The forty long miles of farmland since leaving Darby Creek Park had been particularly trying for me to ride. With the obvious soreness aside, the open miles of farmland dulled my senses and drained my curiosity to explore, that is until I noticed an array of colors from the trailside foliage that visually awakened my stupor. Rather than staring at the seemingly endless fields of corn I started to take notice of the splashes of colors on either side of the trail in front of me. Many were likely nuisance plants or weeds that survived the local spray of pesticides or the churning of the soil each year. The bright fall colors included patches of white; Elderberry, Queen Ann's Lace, a variety of yellows including; the Brown Eyed Suzan, Leaf Cups and Goldenrod. Surprisingly, the noxious thistle with its purple bloom decorated the path as well. Crimson seed pods of the Staghorn Sumac tree hung out of reach in the background of trail. While riding in the early summer I remembered also seeing the white buds of the water bound lilies back in Millersburg along Killbuck Creek and in Peninsula while riding along the Cuyahoga River. Occasionally, I stopped to capture this floral display with my camera in hopes of cataloging and referencing later on. This seemed like a simple endeavor however it became a tedious exercise knowing the many varieties of wildflowers in Ohio. And my capacity to get off and back on the bike each time I found a new specimen.

Xenia came about quicker than expected. The city name originates from the Greek word for hospitality and I noticed the city's welcoming vibe as I passed through Shawnee Park. This is a city of many surprises with numerous bike trails radiating from the train depot. Because of this, Xenia has earned the nickname of "The Bicycle Capital of the Midwest". Xenia, and the larger Greene County, is also an area of important historical significance and the source of my intrigue for many years.

As I embarked on this cross-state journey, I was determined to spend time actually reading the state historical markers that are commonly found along the roadside. So many times in the past, during business or pleasure travel, I casually drove by, thinking to myself what might have happened in this area but never taking the time to get out and explore. In the planning stages of this ride across Ohio, I committed myself to stop, photograph, and read each state marker that was within sight of the trail. Deep within the description of each marker was a local point of interest, a person of note, or an event that occurred in the general vicinity of the marker. At a bicyclist's pace, this was the perfect time to explore the deeper meaning and historical significance described on the marker that helped shaped the state. A full listing of each marker found en route along the OTET is provided in the appendix.

Having lived near Xenia for a number of years, I had come to know of its historical importance and was quite certain I would find much more while riding on a bike at a slower pace. In this regard, Xenia certainly did not disappoint. As an aspiring adventurer, I had read many books about the noteworthy pioneers of the early 18th century. Their stories of pursuit and conquest had left a trail of curiosity for me to rediscover. On my bucket list was a desire to become more acquainted with my boyhood heroes, famous pioneers' Daniel Boone and Simon Kenton. As it turned out, Xenia was a significant crossing territory for both as they traveled up and down the Ohio River Valley and into Kentucky for seasonal hunting.

To my surprise, Xenia boasted a sizable historical center known as the Greene County Historical Society, which claims possession to numerous artifacts of this early American lifestyle. This was an opportune time for me to reacquaint myself with this region's history. While waiting for the museum to open in the morning, I took the opportunity to walk around a nearby reconstructed, two-story log cabin. I admired the careful dovetailing of the logs at its corners and the white contrasting mortar used as fill for the aged cracks between each member. The wafting aroma of the well-maintained herb garden framed by a stone walkway gave an ambiance of a well thought out existence and sense of permanence.

Returning promptly at 10:00am, I met with the historical society's director, Catherine Wilson at the door and commented on the beautiful restoration of the log cabin out front. We talked for a while as I explained the purpose of my visit with a specific interest in Simon Kenton and Daniel Boone's history. Catherine was nice enough to give me a personalized tour and started the conversation with her lifelong residence in Xenia and her distant familial connection to Daniel Boone. I thought to myself, well, if you're going to discuss history why not discuss it with a family member. From the center room, Catherine was able to point to different sections of the two-floor gallery and described the area I had the most interest in–the early pioneer section.

Through an earlier Internet search, I learned that the Xenia museum had housed the flintlock rifle used by Simon Kenton. Actually, seeing this relic became one of the latest additions to my bucket list. Having read a great deal about Kenton's marksmanship and legendary skill with the gun, I had built a Christmas morning-like anticipation to seeing the actual article. I tried to contain my enthusiasm for seeing the gun as Catherine went on about Xenia's history. Finally, unable to contain my curiosity any longer, I asked if she knew anything about the Kenton rifle. Despite the fact that I may have used my outside voice a bit too much, she kindly replied, "Oh, but of course. It's in my office". We made our way to her office, which was just a few steps from where we were standing. The gun, housed in its own deep frame, was hanging over her desk. For an old Kenton fan, it was like finding a lost puzzle piece and filling the final hole in the picture. Very satisfying.

To my surprise, just below the rifle hung another deep frame that housed a primitive jackknife, half opened to display the blade. The entirety of the knife was eight inches in length. On the handle was an inscription; DBOON. Indeed, I was looking at another piece of history, this one carried by the great Daniel Boone. Catherine described how the gun and knife were received as a gift through the James Galloway family. Galloway had been an early resident of Greene County and the builder of the admirable, early 1800s era cabin that sat in front of the museum. Galloway had befriended both Kenton and Boone as a matter of survival while mapping early Greene County. After having taken a few pictures of the gun and knife, we both took a walk to the Galloway cabin where the articles had been originally housed. As we crossed through the herb garden, I had to ask Catherine why the gun was on display in her office. Surely, a relic such as this deserves a prominent home in the center of the museum. Catherine responded that, subsequent to an incident a few years back, they liked to keep it under multiple security systems.

Walking through the Galloway cabin, Catherine described that the structure had been moved three times before making its way to its present location. She added that it had also seen a number of restorations and presently contained about 70% of its original logs. I learned that Galloway was one of the first settlers of the area and started the early survey work for what is now known as Greene

County. As Catherine described Galloway's history, I envisioned this simple two-floor structure becoming a secure meeting point for early pioneers to exchange tales of their travels and tribulations during a rather untamed and downright dangerous time for early settlers.

On the way back to the museum, Catherine became more relaxed as we realized that we had many periods of common historical interest. Possibly pushing the "too inquisitive" side of every conversation, I found Catherine's occupation as the proprietor of a small museum rather intriguing. Catherine not only had an interest in the local history but was also an actual part in this history as she described another monumental event in Xenia's past. The year was 1974 and, as a young girl of nine, she and her siblings were quickly rushed to the family bathtub as a dark and ominous cloud gathered. What happened in the next half hour resulted in the razing of the city of Xenia. Being at the tail end of tornado alley, Xenia was not accustomed to tornados or certainly what was to happen next. On this particular April day, a category F5 tornado struck Xenia, killing 33 and injuring 1,300 more. Fortunately, for Catherine and her family they all survived. In the years to follow, a sense of obligation to family and local history lead her to become a knowledgeable source of local history and a natural representative of the Xenia and Greene County Historical Society. I had spent more time than I had planned and felt the need to get back on the road again. I told Catherine that I enjoyed every minute of our discussion. In turn, she asked me if I would sign her visitor log and let everyone with whom I come into contact know about this gem of a spot along the Ohio to Erie Trail. Without a doubt, she had my commitment.

Remembering that my cell phone drained its power on the first day of the ride, I had been out of touch with my family for most of the week. Adding insult to injury, I had grabbed the wrong power cord and was unable to charge the phone anyway. Too frugal and too frustrated with the durability of my electronic equipment, I asked Catherine if I could make one telephone call on her landline. Of course, in a museum with marginal funding, the call was on a vintage 1980's style phone; a museum relic in its own right compared to today's technology. The call to my wife of 26 years went as expected.

Road Rule Number Ten
Always leave a trail of where you've been and where you're going.

In the 2000s, a book titled Between a Rock and a Hard Place written by adventurer Aron Ralston describes his survival experience on a rock-climbing trip in Blue John Canyon in Utah. In the course of his trip, his arm became pinched between a sizable rock formation and a large boulder. Ralston found himself unable to extricate his arm from between the two surfaces. Even worse, he was stuck with limited supplies. The following six days became a gripping tale of survival. Aron later admitted that the whole ordeal could have been avoided if he had just let someone know where he was going and how long he planned to be out of town.

The point here is to keep in touch with someone while striking out on a new adventure. Self-reliance is important for all adventurers but an ounce of preparation such as a compiling a travel itinerary or carrying a charged cell phone can save your hide from the unexpected. By the way, I recommend the book, especially if you're an adrenaline junkie.

When on the road alone, it is important to keep your loved ones informed about your movements in the unlikely but altogether possible event that something goes wrong. To my credit, I left a financial trail with the credit card that I had used to purchase food in each town. Though we had not spoken, I knew that Laurie's nature as a financial hawk meant that she was generally aware of my location spending. As for my personal well-being, I had been out of touch for three days and I anticipated that Laurie was fuming over my "off the radar" communication style. True to form, my opening explanation did not justify my lack of communication and I received my due correction. As the call wrapped up, I left word that Cincinnati was within striking distance by the end of the day. I pictured a relatively easy 60-mile ride into Cincinnati where my son, Sean was attending college. I could envision pushing back a couple beers and grabbing a hot shower as Sean and I burned the late hours.

Boy, I couldn't have been more wrong about this projection.

Once I had finished my phone call home, I prepared to head back out on the road but before doing so I asked Catherine one final question. I was curious about the issue with the Simon Kenton gun. She told me that the gun had gone missing in the early 1970s, just before the '74 tornado. The building that originally housed the rifle was demolished along with many other artifacts during the storm. A dozen or so years later, a mysterious call was received from Texas in which the caller asked if the museum was missing an antique muzzleloader. The caller mentioned the Xenia Historical Center property tag, which marked the gun and thought the gun had some historical value. Soon after the gun was returned to its rightful owner and put back on display to be shared with the general public. This little footnote of history made the visit even more compelling and well worth the effort of making a stop.

The next part of the day should have been an easy flat 60-mile day as I traced the Little Miami River into Cincinnati where it gently flows into the Ohio River. The reconstructed Xenia Train Depot now served as the hub of Ohio's bike network, sending riders and pedestrians off in many directions as the paths radiate from the hub. With map in hand and studying my route toward Cincinnati, I chose my trail out of Xenia.

Despite my best efforts to pick the correct trail, the route I chose sent me–incorrectly–northwest towards Yellow Springs rather than south to Cincinnati. Little did I know that the day's difficulties were just beginning as I purposefully headed out of Xenia in the wrong direction.

With a variety of trail options radiating from Xenia, I advise future travelers to take caution and make sure your trail selection matches with your destination. Generally there are attendants at the Xenia Train Depot to provide further clarity. Many miles later on the bike trail, I came across a runner who appeared to be having dehydration issues and was cramping and dry heaving on the side of the path. I stopped to offer her some consolation and water. With two full water bottles carried on the bike frame, I offered the first bottle. The runner was appreciative for the water and the recognition of her situation. She claimed I was an angel in disguise. I had to think twice about this knowing I had been three days on a bike and was pretty pungent smelling for an angel. We continued exchanging running snippets and then she asked where I was heading. I boldly claimed, "Cincinnati" and told her I was planning to arrive that evening. I was dumbstruck when she pointed out on my map that I was heading in the wrong direction. If I continued much further, I would make Springfield, placing me 20 miles in the wrong direction. At this point, I was feeling pretty humiliated and frustrated with my obvious error. Thankfully, this total stranger had saved me from a worse loss of time. I was now feeling like an angel had been sent my way. This little exchange brings to mind the importance of the next road rule.

Road Rule Number Eleven
Be an ambassador for cycling and be nice to strangers.

In other parts of the world where nomadic travel is a way of life, the traveler is an emissary carrying a message of peace or care for one family or another. In eastern Africa, an old Swahili proverb is commonly used to describe the role of the traveler; "Mgeni aje mwenyeji apone". This roughly translates to "When the guest visits, the host is healed". Many miles of travel have exposed me to those with a dream to be untethered from their life conditions, much as a touring cyclist is untethered from the office chair or work routine. As cyclists, we carry a rare trait of optimism no matter the condition. Yes, we can complain with the best of them but when it comes to enduring distress or physical hardship, the cyclist is equipped like no other. The optimism of the next sunny day, the next farmer's market (and the opportunity to gorge on food), or the next downhill cruise is always around the next corner and often are the stuff of which food dreams are made. With this positive outlook on life, the cycling tourist has a rare oppor-

tunity to influence others to experience their surroundings beyond the comfort of a car. The cycling tourist is an ambassador who awakens the possibility that a ride around the block, a ride to the next neighborhood, or a ride across town is achievable. Distant cycling at its core increases the confidence to be self-reliant and go the next mile.

Many years ago while riding through a small farming town in rural Wisconsin, I was coming to the end of a long day with my heavy load on two wheels. I was suddenly startled by a young boy who snuck up behind me on his Stingray bike. He was curious enough to ask, "Where ya going, mister?" As I explained my mission of riding through not just his state but many others as well, he blurted back that he wanted to do that some day. As the chit-chat continued over the next couple of miles, we were as close as two kids dreaming about the future from the end of an old, wooden fishing pier. Shortly thereafter, he sped away. Some distance later, I found his bike on the side of the road. The boy and his family were nearby, out in front of their family farm and grocery. As I passed, they waved me down from their front porch and insisted that I select some fresh fruit and cheese from their grocery. This was a small but welcome bonanza for a calorie-craved cyclist. As I walked away from the barn, a faded sign advertising Colby Cheese caught my eye. As I packed up my bike with cheese, I could not help but wonder if this was part of the famed Colby Cheese family.

I don't know if the young rider ever took his Stingray cycling aspirations beyond the family farm but I do know he learned about dreaming big that day.

I was 15-miles out of Xenia and headed in the wrong direction! I quickly reversed my heading on the path and reassessed my situation. A visit with my son would now take a near heroic effort. Instead of a relaxed 67-mile day, I was looking at another 100-plus mile day. Furthermore, was this middle-aged body physically capable of turning back-to-back centuries? From within, a familiar feeling emerged best described as a controlled rage. The competitor inside immediately woke up for the challenge.

Game on.

With ear buds plugged in and riding in the lower portion of the handlebars, known as the "drops", I returned to Xenia by 12:30pm averaging 15-miles-per-hour. The self-talk along the way was a mix of internal criticism and a rolling calculation factored to achieve the goal of arriving in Cincinnati by nightfall. This was going to be a clear example of brawn over brains that had gotten me out of jams in the past. Stopping at a roadside Subway, I grabbed a tuna foot-long and devoured each section of the sandwich while jamming to some iPod tunes. It was a literal "eat and ride".

Back in Xenia, I came across a group of riders all colorfully dressed in bike jerseys and participating in a multi-day bike tour that was occurring over the weekend. According to the markings on the path, there appeared to be options of 30, 60, and 100-mile rides each, all originating in Xenia. As I was now crossing paths with the returning groups dressed in their polyester event tech shirts designed to commemorate Xenia Bike event, I grinned at my fashion-challenged appearance. Funnier yet were the pieces of lettuce and tuna from the submarine sandwich that had been splattered on my t-shirt while I was eating on the ride. The returning cyclists reminded me of a curiosity of human nature that occurred to me when I was a runner. The challenge is an old social experiment testing the friendly jesters of a total stranger performing the same activity in an opposing direction. While on the road with a steady stream of oncoming cyclists, I had the opportunity to apply some statistical science to the question of whether or not two strangers who are passing one another while traveling in opposite directions will acknowledge or wave to one another. My inference was that the two strangers would likely not greet each other.

As I continued to wave at each rider, I took note of the mixed reaction from the 100 or so riders that passed. The responses ranged from a nod of the head to a returned hand gesture to a "stare straight ahead and ignore the crazy old dude with a four-day growth of beard and an unkempt appearance" type of response. Many riders were wearing headphones and I found the reactions of those riders interesting and similar to the reactions of those in the running community. It was about a 30/30/30 split of acknowledgment including the wave, the verbal, and the snub. This would make an interesting Ph.D. study considering the demographics and environmental variations. Meanwhile, the streaming hodgepodge of bike equipment continued, including hybrids, tandems, faring-equipped, recumbent, and road bikes.

Having occupied my time south of Xenia with my social experiment I had passed through Spring Valley, Corwin and Oregonia in the blink of an eye. Twenty miles had passed and with little distinction between town line or highway overpass, and yet the trail continued on unobstructed. If interested for a deeper emersion in the heartland town of Waynesville there are amenities for the weary traveler located about a mile off the trail. Look for Corwin Avenue crossing the OTET and head west to Waynesville. For the time being, plan on having your water bottles full through this area. Entering Springfield marks the fourth and final segment of the OTET. If following the OTET Touring Guide this is also known as the Southern Region.

As the path continues further south a set of surprisingly large concrete abutments uncharacteristically stand out amongst the wooded river and path. Following these structures hundreds of feet above show the underbelly of the I-71 highway. A short while later, signs for the future site of the Fort Ancient Archeological Park appeared along the trail. This site had largely been an attraction featuring the early Paleo-Ohio civilizations. The Hopewell Indian tribe had ruled up and down the Little Miami River for centuries before European interests began to develop in the east. These tribes occupied the region between 200 BC and 300 AD and found the area plentiful for nourishment and for ease of transportation. After some hard bike miles, I decided to take a side excursion on foot to see this historic site. A small sign on the path gave the impression that a short quarter-mile walk would place me at the ancient site. The short distance became a major undertaking as the uphill climb was on an undeveloped path. My hard-soled bike shoes did not make the task any easier as I struggled to gain traction on my way up the hill.

Finally, on the top and at first glance, Fort Ancient appeared to be a large football field with mounding hills around its perimeter. As I studied the mounds in the open grassy space, I started to make sense of the layout and organization. A quick read of the historical placards tells of a scientific change of thought in which the mounds, originally believed to be some manner of fortification, are now considered to be a large-scale sundial or a modern-day calendar, similar in purpose to England's Stonehenge.

The return trip down the steep embankment proved equally treacherous in my hard-soled shoes as I navigated back through the trail with natural obstacles and loose shale. The descent was complicated as a light drizzle, which had been falling since Xenia, was now turning to rain accompanied by heavy, dark clouds. Returning to my bike, I decided to pedal on as the canopy of trees softened the constant rain. As I made my way, the wind-driven rain became a steady downpour and forced me to pull out my rain gear. Slipping on the bright yellow rain gear allowed my core body temperature to regulate in spite of the rain and provided a shallow sense of security from the eventual soaking.

Oftentimes when alone on the road and with the elements working against me, even a shadow of negativity can dramatically affect my ability to physically and intellectually deal with the real or perceived situation. An old hiker once told me, "As the mind goes so does the body". When faced with these situations, I find it important to maintain a realistically positive perspective of my situation. Once again, an old, favorite song to break the cycle of negative thoughts is in order. In this case, my song of choice was an old REO Speedwagon song, "Keep Pushin". I followed this musical reverie with a near clinical assessment of my condition:

Food? Check.
Core temperature? Check.
Fluids? Check.
Remaining strength? Check.

Undercarriage? Uncomfortable.

Finally, I assessed my environment and equipment. If I can rationally work through these thoughts, I am generally moving in the right direction.

Road Rule Number Twelve
Stop the negative, replace with positive and realistically assess.

When working with the Boy Scouts as a troop leader, we often ended our long days by sitting around a campfire ring and sharing our thoughts about the day's strenuous hike or other events. This exercise was commonly known as "thorns, rose, and buds ". In turn, each scout would reflect on his likes, dislikes, and most importantly the opportunities that each hoped to see, do, or achieve in the coming days. Surprisingly, even on the most strenuous of days and in the most inclement conditions, each scout could dig deep enough to find one ember of hope that would keep him motivated to move forward.

When performing most physical activities, your mind is assessing your body and its performance. On a surface level, it may be a sore knee or a nagging hitch in a running stride. Each of the day's little events or environmental conditions are also continually being assessed and creating a disposition that can range from euphoric and positive to brooding and negative. Whatever the condition, it is important to be in tune with these changes in mood and outlook.

To stay realistically positive is to recognize the negative elements causing your poor outlook and objectively identify a positive outcome with your available skills and resources. Even when your immediate future looks gloomy, assess all of your skills, your resources, and your equipment when trying to determine a course of action that will lead you to a better outcome. Stay calm and generally unemotional. Think through your options, determine your corrections, and don't procrastinate in taking action.

Passing South Lebanon and entering Kings Mills, the famed Kings Island Amusement park can often be heard from the trail.

For the seeker of unique history this park once hosted a young daredevil by the name of Evel Knievel, who electrified the nation with a world record motorcycle jump over fourteen Greyhound busses back in 1975. For all other thrill seekers, the park is a wonderful place to spend the afternoon.

While riding this portion of the scenic section of the OTET there are numerous reminders of its original purpose. The Little Miami Railroad, which was built in the 1840's served to connect the growing industry of Cincinnati with the Capital center in Springfield—Columbus area. The line was in active use until 1981 and was subsequently turned into the Little Miami Bike Trail. Riding this beautifully old tree lined stretch of trail reminds me of the historic events that occurred here. Talking with residents in Loveland and Miamiville there are numerous points where our famed President Lincoln once stayed or stopped while using this very rail line to promote his candidacy for President. Sadly, after Lincoln's election the same line was transporting soldiers to nearby Camp Dennison for the Civil War.

Passing through Loveland and Miamiville has always been a particularly enjoyable portion of the ride for me as the scenic trail passes through old whistle-stop towns that strive to keep the ambience of colonial turn of the century charm. These New England styled community's poised alongside the rail were at one time a popular bedroom community for the booming city of Cincinnati. A 30-minute commute by train made for a hassle-free portage into the city some 100 years ago. Now the town has been carefully transformed into a stop for bikers and other tourists looking for a glimpse of the "good old days". Loveland has done a wonderful job of integrating the bike trail into its community. Rain or shine there is a vibrant sense of activity that provides numerous eating opportunities within eyeshot of the trail.

Traveling another eight miles south from Loveland I rode through a quiet and diffident neighborhood of Camp Dennison. After decades of suburban growth in and around the old rail line, the history of this area is generally obscured by the unknowing traveler. Though not highly visible from the trail there are undulations and earth work reticent of an old train depot foundation, numerous old barns showing decades of weathering each providing clues to the areas prior use. Camp Dennison was an old military recruiting and training center established in 1861, and was used by the Union Army to defend Cincinnati in the event of a Confederate raid. A mere 17 miles from the city troops were able to deploy rapidly by rail or river.

Riding through Camp Dennison, I recognized the familiar signs of a restoration project not more than 50 feet from the path. An old prominent brick house that clearly had seen better days had a few extension ladders and scaffolding carefully positioned against the two-story building. The work at hand appeared to be the removal of rotted wood under the eaves of this classic house. Outside by the front door was a white board advertising "Open House". Curiosity getting the better of me, I hopped off the bike, and leaned it against the crooked black iron fence and walked through the open door. When my eyes acclimated to the dim lighting I was stunned by the openness of the first room. A pair of long waist high countertops adorned each side of the oversized room and shelving lie just behind the counters. The shelves were lined with old mason jars, drinking cups and a variety of common hardware attempting to replicate the scene of an old grocery store was apparent. The front counter prominently displayed an old chrome plated National Cash Register, with a decorative sign displaying the name W.B. Knicely. As I was about to explore deeper into the cavernous room, I heard a voice behind me ask, "do like what you see"? A bit startled I turned around to meet the apparent proprietor, a middle-aged man in jeans and tee shirt covered with saw dust. Having done some home remodeling of my own I responded enthusiastically with interest and engaged in one of the most fascinating tours of historic reconstruction. Willie my host, an exuberant and skilled craftsman, began to take me on a tour of the building that had been carefully restored by hand right down to the window sashes and door frames in order to preserve the original integrity of glass or antique hardware. Artifacts dating to the early 1860's were stored in a window box collaborating a story of this early American relic. The building was purportedly built as officer's quarters during the construction of Camp Dennison. It was later owned and operated by the Knicely family over the next three generations, as a primary residence and General Grocery store until the 1950's. Today it is a lasting legacy and work in progress wanting to regain its significance in Ohio's history. As I thanked Willie for his time and the tour, I returned to my bike thinking there are likely many other gems of history to explore in this area, when time allows.

Shortly after Camp Dennison the towns of Milford and Terrace Park emerged on the path. Conveniently located along side the path is a structure called the Riverwalk Bicycle Barn, a small bike rental provision that also provides basic tools if a mechanical concern ails the rider. Together with a nearby porta-potty, the area caused a bit of congestion on the trail. Otherwise this was a great spot to top off my tires with air and perform a couple of mechanical checks on my bike. As a self-service styled arrangement, pumps and a bike stand were located outside, for anyone who knew what they were doing. Obviously, the mechanically inclined biker would be a popular catch in such an area. Performing a couple of repairs on my bike drew enough attention that I ended up helping two other stranded cyclists. One flat tire and a loose chain fix later I was back on the trail riding.

From my maps I knew that I would soon be approaching Cincinnati and a six-mile segment that would be the final section of city street riding, and needing careful navigation while in traffic. Talking with friends associated with the OTET Fund they are persistently closing the few remaining gaps in the 326-mile trail. At present there are three such gaps of significance and they each occur in the cities of Cleveland, Columbus and Cincinnati. Generally, the cities have presented the most challenge for the trail passage due to property restrictions, physical barriers and financial concerns. While plans or funding are in place for connectors and bridge structures, each will ensure safe passage throughout the OTET system.

The Little Miami Bike Trail portion of the OTET ends in Avoca Park and then carefully routes the rider onto US 50 also known as Wooster Pike Road. During the next six miles a moderate level of traffic through the communities of Mariemont, Fairfax, and Linwood require alertness to all automobile traffic. Knowing the importance of being visible on my bike I got off for a moment to turn my front and rear bike lights on as added measure of safety to my ride. There were few signs differentiating between these active suburban communities, interestingly I could smell food on the grill as I passed numerous establishments reminding me that it was near dinner time. Like an old friend departing, the Little Miami River departs from the OTET near the intersection of Wooster Pike and Meadowlark Roads. With minimal traffic or congestion, the OTET returns back to bike path as Wooster Road terminates at the Lunken Airport.

Returning to the bike path the expansive Ohio River comes into view while passing through Turkey Ridge Park. The Ohio River dwarfs the Little Miami tributary that feeds it, and for the past miles the stark contrast of colorful kayaks and canoes floating on the Little Miami are now replaced by massive freighters carrying their cargo. The Ohio River serves as a thoroughfare to the Mississippi River and points further south west. From Pittsburg to Cincinnati the Ohio River also passes through Indiana, Illinois and Kentucky. Standing by the river's edge I watched a couple of cargo ships silently pass by as they transported their goods floating west.

The southern terminus of the OTET is at the John Roebling Bridge, a short six miles from the Lunken Airport. Along the way are carefully manicured parks and gardens amplifying the openness of the city by the river's edge. A light breeze bends the decorative grasses, and colorful plantings which adorn the path. Along the river's edge are a succession of historical markers that that tell the story of the assorted immigrant groups that helped to build the city and its diverse communities. I decided to take pictures of each and read the interesting details later for the benefit of those who might want to explore further. A summary of these historical markers along the entire trail are cataloged in the appendix.

While casually riding along the Ohio River taking pictures and reading about the local history the bike path was still a few hundred yards from the river. As with dipping my wheel in the Lake Erie water and the states northern boundary I wanted to commemorate the completion of the OTET by dipping the same wheel in the Ohio River. Finding my first opportunity to do this appeared as the bike trail passed under the I-471 Overpass. Nearby, the river's edge in Yeatman's Cove a pair of large red steam boat paddle wheels were artistically suspended upon stanchions simulating extensive drive mechanics that once propelled the great paddle wheel boats nearly a century ago. I carefully rolled my bike down a sloping cobblestone pad that also served as a parking lot to the water's edge. Gently I nudged the front tire in and claimed a small personal victory; "Across Ohio State-border to border, 326-miles, same bike, same legs". Satisfied with the accomplishment and mentally checking the "bucket list" I was ready to give my son Sean a call to get cleaned up and have a few laughs over dinner.

After a satisfying dinner Sean and I briskly walked back to his dorm room before we called it a night. We discussed tomorrows travel, putting me back on the OTET to Xenia and to points further north along the Miami Valley Trail to a familiar part of the state we once called home. This excursion would be another long ride but would pass through familiar areas of Dayton, Tipp and finally ending in Troy. As the rain continued to beat against the window pane, my last thought before dozing off, was that I had picked a good night to be inside under solid shelter, rather than tenting in the rain. Such is the gamble of travel by bike.

Finishing the OTET in Cincinnati closed a chapter of curiosity and exploration between the state boundaries for me. Though my preferred method of travel is to be self-sufficient and to camp along the trail, this requires a level of rigor not shared by many other cyclists. While traveling with the OTET Fund raiser group recently, I developed an appreciation for another form of cycle travel which was affectionately referred to by the group as Glamping; a cross of glamor and camping. This form of travel accommodates for the mobility of the cyclists as well as the overnight glamor of a freshly made bed each night, possibly food service along the way, and the relief of not carrying all that gear.

Knowing that there is a planned destination at the end of each day adds a sense of security and protection from the elements or unfamiliar surroundings that many travelers would prefer not to deal with. Glamping does require a degree of advanced planning and coordination that is generally managed by a ride leader or an event planner. If you are more accustomed to the small group or solo initiatives there are numerous options of overnight accommodations near the OTET that will enable the cyclists to enjoy the trail. In the Appendix section of this book are a series of charts providing the traveler with a number of camping and non-camping options along the OTET, based on your desired pace and comfort. As with most hotels, lodges or bed and Breakfasts options each offer different levels of accommodations. Those listed in the Appendix were selected based on ease and access to the OTET, affordable pricing, and distance to other services and food options. Some of the B&B's have a limited number of bed options and I would recommended a 6 month advance reservation when choosing this option.

Day Five
Cincinnati to Troy - 105 miles

Enjoying the day's first coffee at a local campus shop, I began jotting down the previous day's notable events in my journal while Sean worked at his summer job on the golf course. As the pedestrian traffic ambled by the front window, this quiet time allowed me to get my thoughts committed to paper. Deep in thought, a curious young man casually approached and introduced himself as Preston, an English major who was teaching at a local high school. As a side vocation, he also assisted inexperienced writers in composing and editing their heart-felt journals of thought and intrigue into a formal publications. As one example, he described a drug addict who made good on his life after an unfortunate beginning and a conversion to Christianity. Now a productive contributor to society, this former drug addict is working with at-risk inner-city kids to prevent the same experiences from occurring in their lives.

I showed Preston the map of the Ohio to Erie Trail and he showed a genuine interest in the trip. This interest started my creative juices flowing about my adventure travels and my aspirations to publish the travel notes one day. We casually discussed the publishing process for a while and he left me with some ideas to ponder in the future. Though I never thought of myself as a writer, Preston's comments planted a seed that one-day might bear fruit. If you're reading this now in a formal publication, we can credit Preston for the motivation. Like Preston, many of the other people I've met during my travels bring to mind Road Rule Number 13. The casual and random acquaintances we make each day may redirect a destination or crystalize an inner passion.

Road Rule Number Thirteen
Meet someone interesting daily. Allow conversations to develop. These are the gems of the day.

When I first biked across the country as a young man, the bike and the travel became a vehicle for seeing national parks and recognizable sights. Looking back after 30-years of travel by bike, I realized that I missed a sizeable portion of self-discovery and purpose for the ride. Replaying the mental tape many years later, the memories that come back in full color are the people that I met and the impressions that they left on me. Don't get me wrong; the photographs and postcard images are all equally beautiful and serene but the brief acquaintances with other human beings carries an emotional context that remains etched in our memory for years afterward.

With many miles of cycle travel behind me, I have experienced highs and lows from each and what I have concluded to be the most memorable achievements are not the places I've been nor the miles I've ridden nor the pain I have endured. The memories most cherished are those that involve human contact and the brief exchange of ideas with people from different backgrounds.

It was at about this point that Sean joined Preston and me having returned from the golf course and it was time for me to return to the bike trail. We each polished off our remaining cups of coffee and I carefully picked up my maps and wished Preston good luck with his endeavors as he returned the salutation.

Today's travel plan is to head north to Troy retracing the Miami Valley Bikeways trail up to Xenia and then take a north-west branch towards Dayton. Returning to the point where I dipped the bike tire in the river yesterday Sean and I stood on the banks of the Ohio River. Gazing in both directions we attempted to grasp the size and enormity of the great river. Across the river on the Kentucky side, we spied a vintage river boat equipped with its large, red paddle wheel positioned at the rear of the boat. This was one of the earliest forms of motorized propulsion used to travel up and down these waterways. Originally powered by compressed steam, later models were powered by diesel engines, which served to propel the boat through the water. These relics from the late 1800's are used today to support a popular tourism trade in this region. A couple of boats could be seen unloading passengers on the Kentucky side. We continued to walk further along the river parkway toward the massive stanchions of the John Roebling Bridge. These impressive structures tower high above the river on both sides. The John Roebling Bridge is an early example of a suspension bridge designed by its namesake. Two massive buttresses made of local sandstone flank either side of the Ohio's edge and are connected by long spans of bundled cable, painted in a shade of light blue.

The Roebling Bridge stands today, as one of the country's first suspension bridges. This iconic bridge was completed in 1866 as the first major connector between Ohio and Kentucky. At the time of completion, this was the world's longest suspension bridge, boasting a span of just over 1,000 feet in length. The bridge carries many similar features of its famous sister to north east, the Brooklyn Bridge, which was constructed by Roebling's son 30-years later. As we walked around the historic bridge, I reflected on the familial connection of these two historic bridges.

Returning to the Xenia Train Depot was exactly as I had left it yesterday. I carefully read all my maps and took note of Road Rule Number Six again; *Let go of the electronics, use your surroundings, and use your senses.* I certainly did not want a repeat of yesterday's misdirection debacle and so I carefully double checked my routing, and headed northwest to Dayton. Despite yesterday's wet and raw finish, there were a few complaints from the undercarriage department and I remembered a little saying, "discomfort is the origin of resilience". And with this in mind I started to find the day's cadence and was feeling pretty good about the-day's effort ending in Troy. After 20-miles or so, I approached the Riverside - Linden Township line. The trail narrowed and took an unexpected hard right-hand turn but there was a lack of trail change markings. I took note of the turn and continued left in a southwest direction that appeared to be the main trail. Within a mile of this intersection, it became evident that I had incorrectly chosen my trail option. Unfortunately, my surroundings took a turn for the worse and they did not pass the "safety gut check"–on a bicycle no less. Odd as it may seem, the environment made me feel uncomfortable, like some kind of threat was around the next turn. I did not want to get lost in this area so I quickly whipped out the maps to regain my bearings. On the proverbial "other side of the tracks", indicators of danger lurked. Garbage caught in the sewer drain, nearby brush littering the lawns, broken bottles in the street, and the rank smell of urine lingering in the air all suggested neglect. While riding on this divergent path, I approached a middle-aged woman slowly churning the pedals of a rusty old, single-speed Stingray bike. She was clearly oversized for the bike as she hunched over the handlebars with her knees nearly hitting her chin. As I came up from behind, I offered my traditional salutation. When she looked up at me I was aghast by her distressed face, almost in tears, with what looked to be a fresh black eye. Shocked by this sight, I squeaked out a meager offering of help as I assumed it was violence-related based on the general surroundings. I did not get much of a response as she continued to push the pedals and wanted no part of a conversation with me. I did not have a lot to offer other than water and possible empathy, not that I looked like an EMT or any other caregiver for that matter. She was clearly on a different planet and wanted no part of mine. I continued on, wondering how else I could have reached her.

All within a short mile of my ill-fated heading, I made my correction and started cycling back to the missed trail change. The distraught cyclist now was nowhere to be found as she had apparently disappeared into the gloomy fabric of neglect found in this rundown part of town. As I retraced my route, I passed some old factory buildings and found one bright spot amongst the scenes of dilapidation. Some rather gifted and creative artists had turned an otherwise depressed area into a brilliant array of color and messaging on the surrounding buildings. Even though empty spray paint cans littered the ground, there was clearly talent in this graffiti. In fact, I felt some of the art was worthy of an exhibit at New

York's Museum of Modern Art. Panel after panel of bold, colorful letters delivered a somewhat cryptic message, making little or no word sense that I could recognize.

With the general condition of the neighborhood and a new bike path cutting through this area, there is a hope that one day a positive light will shine on this neglected part of town. Clearly, the bike trail intends to cut across the fabric of Ohio. This often times takes in the natural beauty of the state and occasionally serves as a harsh reminder of the reality associated with poverty and neglect, not only our in state but our country as well. It is for these experiences that bike travel serves as an awakening and is sometimes coupled with the responsibility to help improve what is wrong.

Having lived in the Dayton area, I took the opportunity to see some of the sights of a recently re-imagined waterfront park along the Great Miami River. The park included water fountains, gardens, and bike paths comparable but smaller to the ones in Cincinnati. Additionally, a number of memorials honoring two of Dayton's favorite inventors, Wilbur and Orville Wright commemorate their achievements within sight of the bike path. The path conveniently follows the Mad River into the city and crosses under a pedestrian bridge that takes a northern tack along the Little Miami River.

Familiar with the area I took an alternate trail from the north-south passage along the Great Miami that allowed me to view numerous historic landmarks made famous by the brothers back in the early 1900's. My trip was not complete without a quick stop on the west side of Dayton and the site of the original bike shop used by Wilber and Orville which doubled as the first working airplane shop. A block away was the foundation of their family home. With Ohio's license plate boasting "The Birthplace of Aviation", Dayton is surely its epicenter. As a quick historical footnote, the title of "Aviation's Birthplace" is commonly contested by North Carolina. With its Atlantic coast location and constant wind, the North Carolina city of Kitty Hawk was the location where the brothers first lifted into the sky in their heavier-than-air flying machine and into history. If time is available I highly recommend a side trip to visit the Wright Brother's Dayton home and bike shop, as well as the Wright-Patterson Air Force Base and Museum, each chronicling the many advances in aviation that have been made in the past one-hundred years.

As I returned from my little foray and back to the north-south branch of the bike trail in Dayton, I passed one of a number of circular concrete abutments about eight feet in diameter. The towering metal structures atop each footing point skyward. Together these structures commemorate Dayton's recovery from the Great Flood of 1913. The haunting memory of the New Orleans flood in 2005 quickly comes to mind when recalling Dayton's tragic early twentieth-century event. The city's precarious location within the Miami River floodplain with its marginal levees became the Achilles' heel for this budding industrial city. A late-night March storm and the convergence of four separate river systems into the Great Miami River resulted in 20 feet of water flooding the city's main streets by 1:30am the next day. Three hundred people in Dayton alone lost their lives as the chilly snow's melt grabbed any structure within its path and breached the existing embankments.

In the wake of this epic flood and $100 million dollars in damage-two billion in today's dollars Ohio's Governor James Cox vowed that the city would never flood again and created one of the nation's first flood control programs and commission. Traveling north, an extensive network of levees, storage basins, and dams have been created and designed to channel excess water. A short journey north from Dayton will take riders over the Englewood Dam, creating the steepest climb for the day and a prime example of the enormity of this undertaking. Since the Governor's original proclamation and years of earthworks the city has successfully engineered a water management program that has since diverted any reoccurring flooding in Dayton.

Following the Great Miami River north, the bike path meanders alongside a gentler pace of water flow. Through the trees that line the river, another causality of the Great Flood can be seen and is commemorated with a historic marker along the bike path. The Town of Tadmor, a once vibrant whistle-stop town, was literally wiped off the map during the flood of 1913. Remnants of old stone bridge foundations, carriage pathways, and foundation building blocks of houses can be seen a short distance from the path. It's just another painful reminder of Mother Nature's fury, when horse path, canal, and train served this budding community a hundred years earlier. Tadmor is now just a Midwest version of a vacant ghost town.

The bike path continues to parallel the Miami Canal system providing a historical reminder of the prosperous cities alongside the canal. The communities of Tipp City, Troy, and Piqua each started as strategic outposts for early pioneers. The fertile soil of the Miami River Valley was recognized for its fruitful farming soil attracting more people in search of a better livelihood. A canal boat once used for delivery service can be found on display along the path in Tipp City. Though many of the canals are overgrown with trees and brush, it is still possible to make out the channels shape and size carved by hard manual labor. The bike paths are likely traversing on the embankments once used as retaining walls for the water flowing through the canal. During the period of the big dig, these towns once served as home to hundreds of immigrant workers who dug the canals by hand. One observer documented that no less than 50 men in a row pushing wheelbarrows to the embankments of the canal could be seen from his perch. Small communities grew into larger ones as the development of canal, rail, and automotive travel quickly outpaced one another. It was now possible to transport produce from field to table in half the time and over increasingly longer distances. Improvement in transportation lowered product cost and increased the development of commerce along the western side of the state. By the mid-1830's, Ohio was the third most populous state in the country preceded by New York and Pennsylvania, each of which was also building canals.

Troy is approximately five miles north of Tipp City along the bike path. In many locations, the Erie Canal and its feeder river, the Great Miami, border the bike path. This western branch was also known at the time as the "Miami Canal" in an effort to distinguish it from its eastern sister, the Ohio Canal. Along the path, a couple of great examples of lock chambers can be seen showing the finish stonework and joinery techniques of the times. Generally, these chambers were 90 feet in length and 15 feet in width and could accommodate a single boat measuring 85 feet by 14 feet. These long boats could carry up to 50 tons of cargo each. As each boat passed through the locks, a toll was sure to be collected. Many long boat operators traveled day and night with the crew and mules taking shifts.

As the path continues through Troy, a large, open field with a red barn at one end is home to the WACO (sounds like taco) airfield. This site boasts the first commercial aircraft runway with its production plants nearby. The Weaver Aircraft Company of Ohio got its start in 1919, soon after the Wright Brothers conquered the sky. The aircraft industry was starting to take off (pun intended), and WACO had developed a sturdy biplane, predominantly used by businessmen and the postal service. During World War II, the company converted their facilities to build gliders that were then notably used during the D-Day invasion of Normandy.

The path gently crosses back and forth over the river as it traverses through Troy. Soon, the high school football stadium comes into view and is the present site for one of the oldest high school football rivalries in the country dating back to 1899 with rival high school, Piqua, to the north. This Midwest Friday night event has gone back and forth for, at last count, 130 times with each side boasting 62 wins a piece (and 6 ties). In full disclosure, Troy was home for our family and many of our friends still live just on the other side of the river from the stadium. If time allows, Troy is a great spot to grab a bite to eat and walk the friendly midwestern streets where today the town is known for its pleasant disposition and core family values.

10-miles to the north of Troy sits another city of historical importance where westbound settlers and the indigenous Indian tribes of the area were commonly in conflict with one another. The city of Piqua, formerly known as Fort Piqua, (circa. 1747), became an early pioneer settlement along the Little Miami River. Because of its location along the popular trade route of the Miami River, the occupying British outpost found itself increasingly under attack by the Eastern Woodland Indian Tribes. These skirmishes in Fort Piqua and other locations within the Miami Valley increased in intensity and later become part of what is now known as the Indian Wars. In the early 1800s, when the area was under American control, the government commissioned John Johnston as an Indian agent to this region.

While in this role, Johnston renewed relations between the warring factions of Indians and incumbent pioneers through cooperative trade and commerce. He built up the local agriculture while maintaining the peace in this prosperous western Ohio boundary outpost. Today, the legacy of Johnston's efforts as an agent, farmer, canal commissioner, and statesman can be explored at The Johnston Farm and Indian Agency Museum. This living museum and site of historical significance serves the community as a cultural reminder of its history in which a difficult past grew into a thriving community.

Today, Johnston's Farms serves as a significant gathering site for "Pioneer Days", bringing artisans of the older, skilled trades together for a reunion of this great era. In recent years, Piqua has also developed a network of bike paths, known as the Linear Loop Park. For years, Piqua has embraced cyclists and pedestrians of many types to share in their history and enjoy life along the canals. With coffee as the primary motivator for this cyclist, I always recommend to other cyclists to stop at Winan's Chocolates. They serve up a great cup of coffee, hot or cold and, if you care to indulge in this third-generation family delicacy (and my personal favorite), the seasonal chocolate-covered strawberries or Ohio's favorite, the Buckeye, which is a chestnut looking candy with a delicious peanut butter center covered in chocolate. Trust me; don't worry about the calories. If you've made it this far on bike, you've earned a treat.

As of this writing, the north-south branch of the Miami Valley Bikeway finds its end in Piqua. The local and regional city commissions to the north are each working to secure property easements within city jurisdiction and, in time, are intent on connecting each together for further pathways. With travels through GOBA and other group rides, there are many more cities to visit on the way north to Lake Erie.

Nearing the day's end and feeling satisfied with the day's work, I decided to head back down the trail from which I came; back to Troy. Knowing the wooded trails well, I was content to set up camp for the night alongside the bike path and jot a few notes in my journal before the sun went down. Strolling through the familiar streets of Troy and down memory lane, I decided to make a quick surprise visit to a friend's house to refresh my water bottles.

As with most friends in Troy, a casual knock on the garage door was the normal approach for familiar faces to announce their presence. Quickly, my friends Joe and Laurie came to the door and ushered me to the backyard where the intoxicating smell of barbecued chicken on the grill filled the air. They were entertaining guests this Sunday evening and insisted that I join them and their guests for dinner. They demanded that I scrap my plans for a water fill-up and instead put a glass of wine in my hands.

How could I refuse?

Hours later, a hot shower, a bellyful of food, and a bed brought this day to a soft ending.

At the pace of a touring cyclist, each is open to exploration at the rider's desire. The people of Ohio, the history of Ohio, and the scenery of Ohio are each a study of dynamic change in their own right. Woven together, a patchwork of creative ingenuity, solid core values, hard work, and available resources, results in a quilt of midwestern values.

Epilogue

How to plan your ride across Ohio?

The writing of *A Path Through Ohio,* 2017 introduces the reader to a variety of riding styles ranging from an individualist's pursuit to a group setting. Between these boundaries are a variety of other options for long distance cyclists. Traveling alone or in a group is an intensely personal decision and requires the rider to constantly analyze their capabilities and desires while on the road. The elements of planning and executing your own tour through all the undulations of success and failure is a thrill generally reserved for the robust and experience traveler. However, on the other end of the spectrum, traveling in a group, or pairing with an unexpected acquaintance provides a level of enjoyment, safety and fun, that occurs while riding as a mobile community. Each ride is an opportunity to explore your confidence and resilience as a distance cyclist. For the unindoctrinated cyclist the OTET is a safe and enjoyable entry into the world of cycle touring. The hills are localized to Homes County, the path conditions are well maintained, the maps and directional cues clear, and local people on the trail are largely welcoming and supportive of bike travelers.

While writing *A Path Through Ohio,* I have had the privilege to ride in a variety of group and solo ride settings with friends and other adventurers of many capabilities and backgrounds. Behind the vail of a successful trip lies hours, weeks and months of careful coordination and planning, making each trip a success. The details of gaining commitments, aligning schedules, reservations and unifying equipment, resources all takes deliberate thought and anticipation of risk's while on the road. Through the development, participation and execution of numerous bicycle travels, I was inspired to create two more Road Rules now numbers fourteen and fifteen, to characterize the importance of developing a solid strategy and to know when to hold firm or to deviate from your plan.

Road Rule Number Fourteen, "Dream it - Plan it - Practice it - Do it", focuses on turning a dream or idea into a set of realistic and tangible actions that will help you make progress towards your dream adventure.

Road Rule Number Fifteen, "Define your trip goals in advance but be agile enough to change your goals. Recognizing that plans are simply thoughts and commitments on a piece of paper. The wise traveler should recognize when conditions are unsafe or personal convictions change, and that it is "OK "to change the plan.

The new rules underscore the importance of planning your own "big hairy" adventure, and at the same time provides for allowance to deviate from your plan as you deem necessary.

The Path Through Ohio was originally written with a solo-cyclists approach for adventure, from Cleveland to Cincinnati. With this second edition and the acquaintance of 35 other adventurers; now friends each have completed the trail as part of an annual OTET Fundraiser. During the one week, 326- mile Journey I had the opportunity to talk one on one with many, and learn of their own personal reasons to ride a bike. Within the group were cancer survivors, community leaders, retirees; (don't forget 86 year old Frank), cross country cyclists, educators, veterinarians, insurance agents, National Park Rangers and many more. Each brought a unique perspective to the trail, whether for exercise, to view the Ohio landscape, or to meet new people from different parts of the state, each had an underlying purpose and preferences about riding a bike. While writing this second edition, I've reflected on my travel preferences; my likes and dislikes while on the bike path. This later became a list of necessities to be aware of as you prepare for your next trip, these "Essentials" as I have framed them are important considerations while traveling by bike. Located in the back, these blocks of useful information can be used to determine what is important for your ride.

The purpose of this book is to provide the reader with enough information to make their own decisions on how they might enjoy the OTET or to explore other bike trail options. Practical decisions need to be made about physical stamina the, length of the trip, the time of the year to ride, or the amount of gear to bring. Even the level of overnight comfort you require from sleeping under the stars to a major hotel chain are preferential questions, the short answer of which is... it depends. When planning any bike trip, it's important to rely on what your own past experiences have been on a bike. What did you like, and what did you not like? If I were to sum up my bike travel preferences the trip would look something like this:

> *Riding alone to explore at will for 80 miles a day with my possessions in two bags on the back of my bike. Breezy warm and dry days, cool nights and sleeping under the stars on a bed of pine needles. Riding near water and occasionally experiencing a challenging climb or two, always close to nature. Making new acquaintances at an unpretentious coffee shop or an ice-cream bar, eating with carefree abandon, sharing experiences with another distance rider. Safe and well-maintained roads free from pollution of any kind. Knowing adventure comes in many flavors and is a brief escape from routine and knowing that there is a home to return to once the meandering is complete...*

This description of course is my perfect scenario and characterizes my ideal adventure. Knowing your perfect scenario is important and requires some advanced thought, plan to spend some time visualizing your travels in advance. Your perfect scenario requires choices to ensure your comfort, safety and achievement of your trip goals. Now is the time to pick up your pencil and scratch down your next big adventure on a piece of paper. With a little preparation and some ingenuity, you can plan the details of your own trip or sign-up for a cross-Ohio bike ride and put yourself in the saddle of one of America's premier bike trails.

Each time I have endeavored to ride the entire trail or even just portions throughout the state I am in awe of the progress that is being made in our state. Each of the major cities of the OTET present mapping and navigation challenges. This is of course difficult and tedious work requiring patience and eye to future improvements that can truly make this a safe and traffic free corridor for cyclists, from start to finish. The OTET Fund and website (referenced in the Appendix) is your best source of information to staying current with routing changes or possible construction.

As the OTET continues grow as one of the state's primary arteries of bike travel, so too are plans to rename the OTET as State Bike Route 1 which will later become an integral part of US Bike Route 21, traveling from Cleveland to Atlanta Georgia. Today, riders will find numerous Bike Route 1 markers along the trail conveniently showing the continuity of what was once a patch work of trails throughout the state. Also, you will find an increasing number of intersecting trail systems which expand the riders range into other reaches of the state. One such trail described in *A Path Through Ohio,* on Day five, is the Miami Valley Bikeway that connects out of Xenia and includes the mid-state cities of Dayton, Tipp, Troy and Piqua. There are numerous other trail systems throughout the state each providing a glimpse the region's best kept secrets.

While Ohio boasts a significant contribution to our country's rich and proud history, it simultaneously continues to be on the cutting edge of progress and innovation. While researching for historical context along the OTET, it was clear that there is a great deal more history to uncover as curiosity and interest dictates. Provided in the Appendix is a list of historical markers which were cataloged and photographed while riding along the trail. Though not an all-inclusive list it does provide a summarized view of the state's dynamic background. With more trail additions in the future, other historical points of interest will emerge.

In preparing a thoughtful closing I found the following two assertions to characterize my motivation to ride a bike. Hopefully you find the same insights true during your travels. Ride well and make your dreams a reality.

"Travel by four wheels transports the body.

Travel by two wheels transports the soul."

***Cycling* reverses the trend of consumerism and emphasizes conservation ~ *It* clears the forest of indecision and requires us to make decisions ~ *It* fills the valley of self-worth with hope and confidence ~ *It* makes straight the path of a singular goal.**

Appendix One
Mileage and Services Along the OTET

The following four charts provide distances between each city and community starting from the North Trail Head in Cleveland or from the South Trail Head starting in Cincinnati. Each chart represents one quadrant of the OTET and aligns with www.ohiotoerietrail.org maps, purchased separately. Key services including Bike repair, Restrooms, Food-water, and Lodging have been identified on or near the trail that will help you plan for your OTET travels. A circle is shaded based on the "strength" or ease and access of each service along the trail. A completely shaded circle indicates a strong access or full service, whereas a partially shaded circle represents a partial or distant service. In all cases it is recommended you bring a smart phone and back up battery source while riding. Of course there are no guarantees the service will be open or available at the time of your travel and in some cases a service may change its location as popularity of the OTET increases over time.

North Region (Cleveland to Millersburg)							
Start: Cleveland	Distance Between (Miles)	Cumulative Miles from Cleveland	Cumulative Miles from Cincinnati	Food	Lodging	Bike Shop	Rest Room
Cleveland	0	0	N/A	◕	●	◕	●
Independence	13.5	13.5	323	◕			●
Peninsula	13.5	27	309.5	◕	◑	◑	◕
Akron	14	41	296	◕	◕		
Canal Fulton	20.5	61.5	282	◕		◕	
Massillon	8	69.5	261.5	◕	◑	◕	
Dalton	11.5	81	253.5	◑			
Apple Creek	10.5	91.5	242	◑			
Fredericksburg	6.5	98	231.5	◑			
Millersburg	9.5	105.5	225	◕	◕		●

North Central Region (Millersburg to Westerville)

Start: Millersburg	Distance Between (Miles)	Cumulative Miles from Cleveland	Cumulative Miles from Cincinnati	Food	Lodging	Bike Shop	Rest Room
Killbuck	6	117.5	215.5	◑			
Glenmont	8	123.5	209.5		◔		
Danville	12	131.5	201.5	◔			●
Mount Vernon	16	143.5	189.5	●	●	◕	●
Mt Liberty	9	159.5	173.5			◕	
Centerburg	5	168.5	164.5	◕			
Sunbury	12.5	173.5	159.5	◕	●		
Galena	2.5	186	147	◑			
Westerville	8	188.5	144.5	◑		◕	●

South Central (Westerville to Xenia)							
Start: Westerville	Distance Between (Miles)	Cumulative Miles from Cleveland	Cumulative Miles from Cincinnati	Food	Lodging	Bike Shop	Rest Room
Columbus	14.5	196.5	136.5	●	●	◕	
Georgesville	12	211	122				◕
London	12.5	223	110	◑	◔		◕
South Charleston	10	235.5	97.5	◑	◕		
Cedarville	11	245.5	87.5	◑			●
Xenia	8	256.5	76.5	◑	●	◕	●

South Region (Xenia to Cincinnati)							
Start: Xenia	Distance Between (Miles)	Cumulative Miles from Cleveland	Cumulative Miles from Cincinnati	Food	Lodging	Bike Shop	Rest Room
Spring Valley	7	264.5	61.5		◔		
Corwin-Waynesville	8	271	53.5	◑	◕		
Morrow	14	279	39.5	●			
Loveland	14	293	25.5	●		◕	
Milford	9	307	16.5	◑		●	
Cincinnati	16.5	323.5	0	●	●		◑

Appendix Two
Maps

The following panels have been selected from the OTET Touring Guide providing directional clarity during the city sections of the OTET. Each of the three C's: Cleveland, Columbus and Cincinnati are actively developing bike trails through a variety of water views, urban parks, and historically significant points of interest. The following maps are titled with city name and map codes aligned with the OTET quadrant maps. N (North Region), NC (North Central Region), SC (South Central) and S (South). A brief description of each section is provided on the following pages to assist the rider through the city roads of the OTET. A complete set of color panels can be purchased at ohiotoerietrail.org.

Map creation by Bob Niendthal

CLEVELAND – EDGEWATER PARK, NORTH TRAIL HEAD (N1)

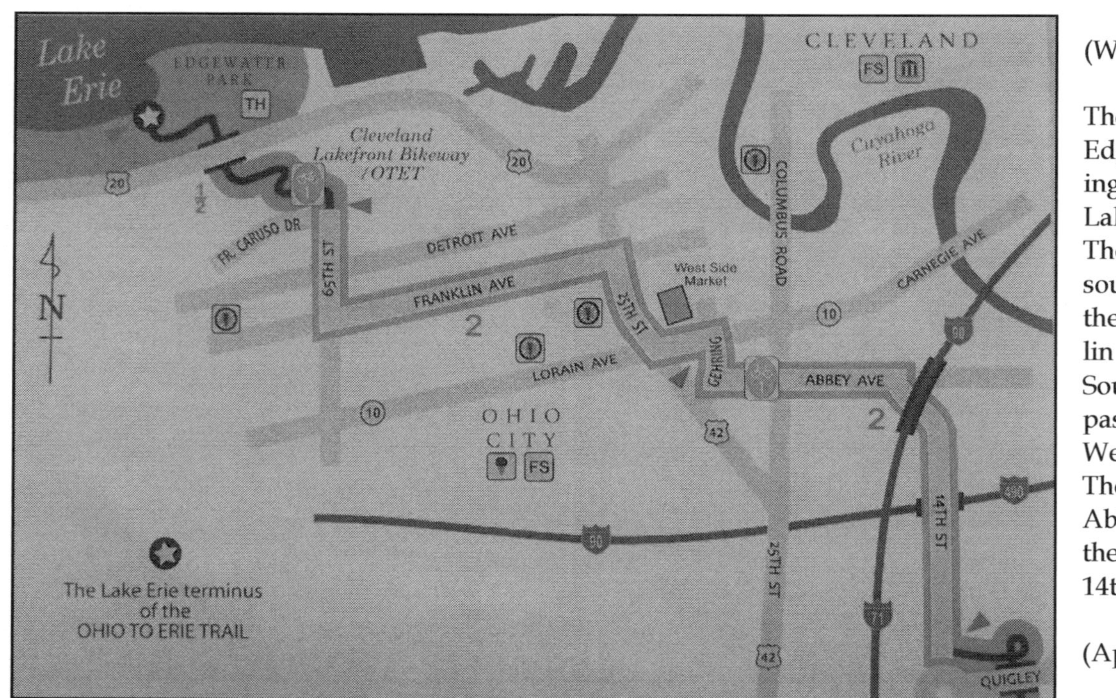

(West to East)

The trail leaves Edgewater Park using the Cleveland Lakefront Bikeway. The OTET travels south on 65th Street then East on Franklin Avenue, then South on 25th Street, passing Cleveland's West Side Market. The route traverses Abby Avenue and then south on 14th.Street.

(Approx. 4.5 miles)

CLEVELAND TO INDEPENDENCE (N2)

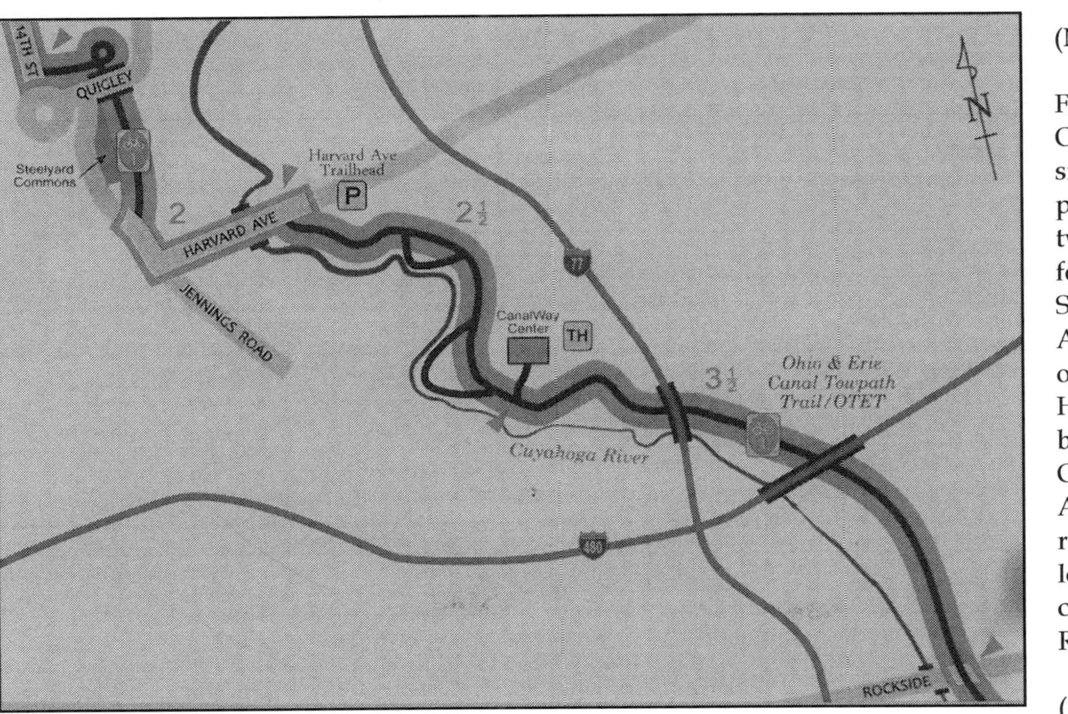

(North to South)

From 14th Street the OTET goes down a significant hill on a paved path through two short tunnels before coming out to the Steelyard Commons. A few hundred yards on Jennings Road then Harvard Avenue brings the Trail to the OTET Canal Towpath. A couple of restaurants are conveniently located as the OTET crosses under Rockside Road.

(Approx. 8 miles)

COLUMBUS (SC1)

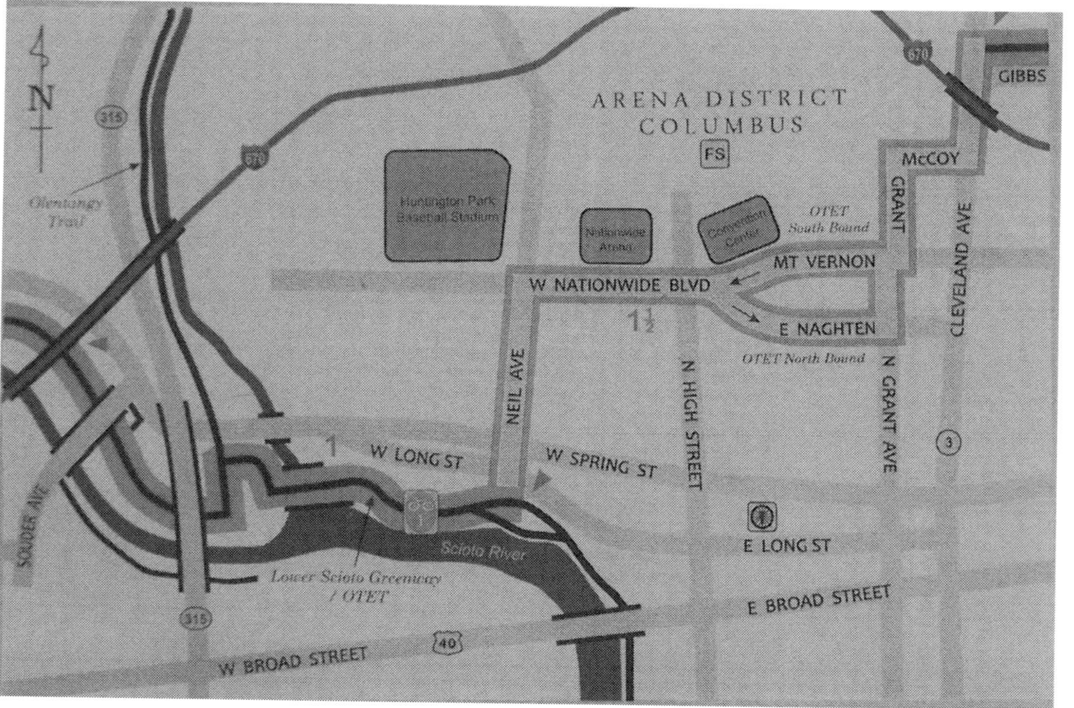

(East to West)

Entering the Arena District of Columbus the OTET follows a short street route for approximately 1.5 miles. After Neil Avenue the OTET follows the Scioto River. Use caution at the T-intersection to ensure your passage continues under Route 315 and follows the Lower Scioto to the Greenway.

(Approx. 2.5 miles)

COLUMUBS (SC2)

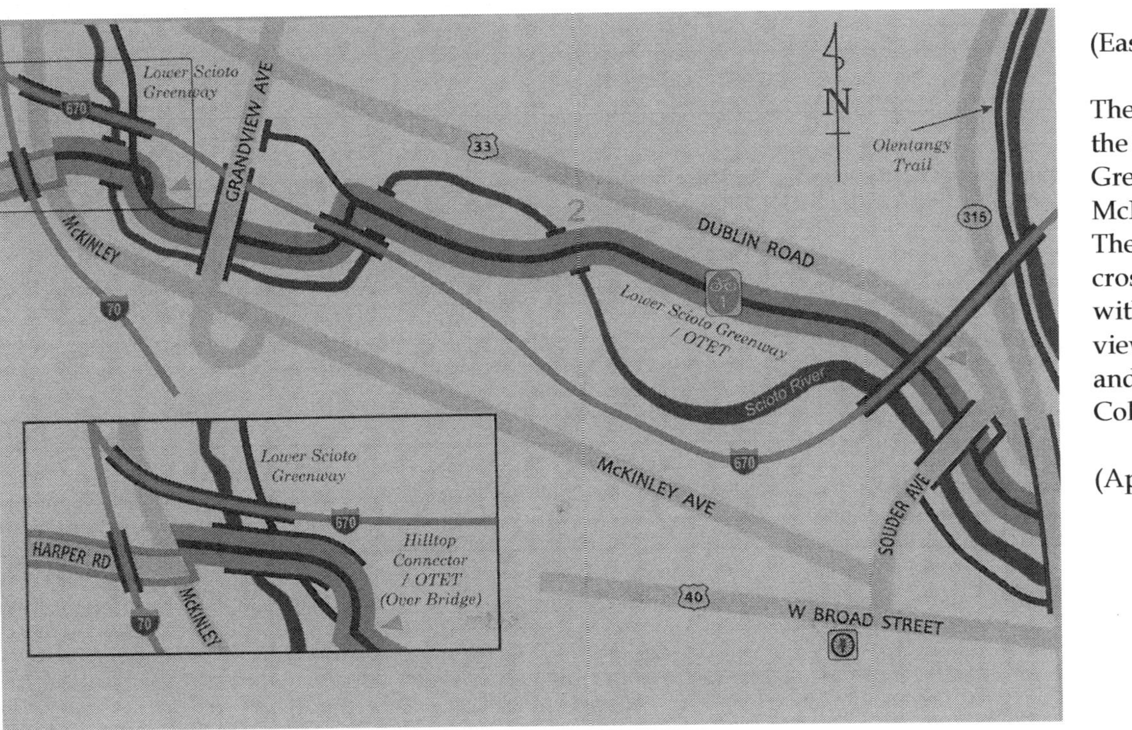

(East to West)

The OTET follows the lower Scioto Greenway to McKinley Avenue. The Scioto River is crossed a few times with spectacular views of the river and Downtown Columbus.

(Approx. 3 miles)

COLUMBUS (SC3)

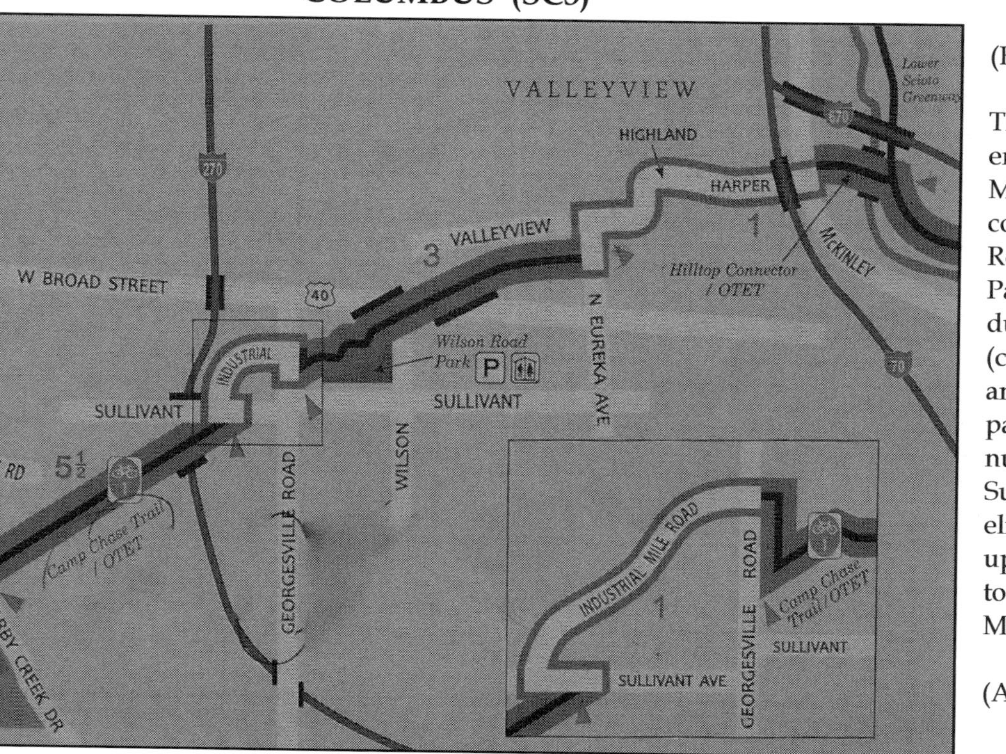

(East to West)

The OTET leaves Lower Scioto Greenway at McKinley Avenue and continues onto Harper Road. The OTET Bike Path continues to Industrial Mile Road (city road) for 1 mile and returns to bike path on Sullivant Avenue. Turn left (east) on Sullivant Avenue traveling 330 feet to pick up the bike path going towards Darby Creek Metro Park.

(Approx. 10.5 miles)

CINCINNATI (S4)

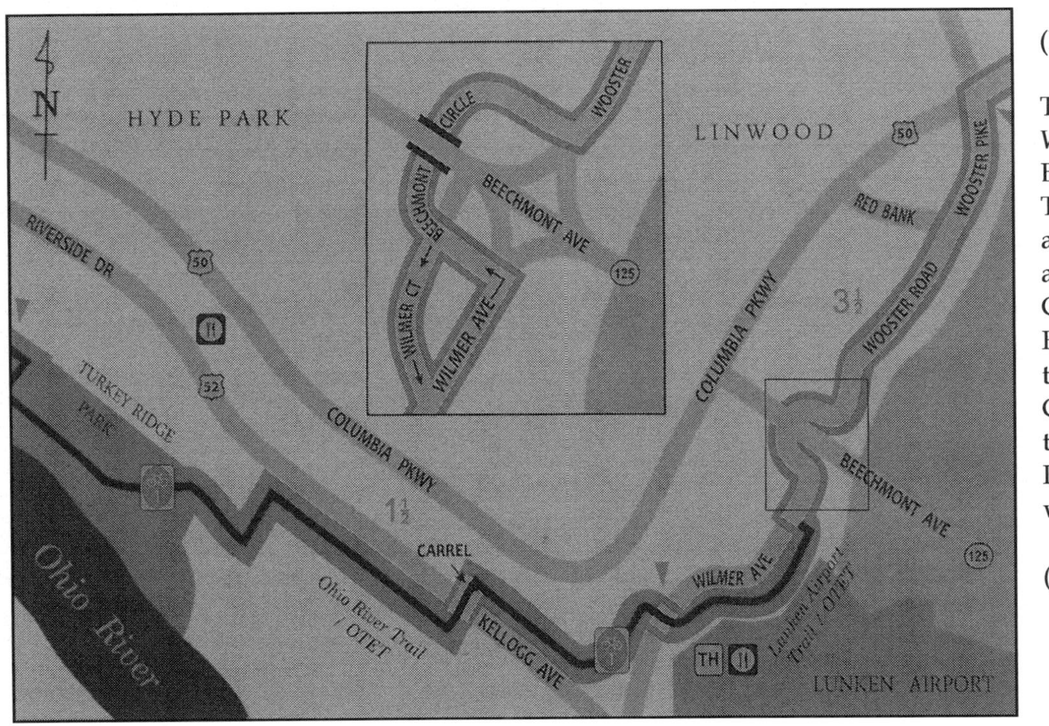

(East to West)

The OTET travels on Wooster Pike/Road to Beechmont Avenue. The bike trail returns at the Lunken Airport, and the Reeves Golf Course parking lot. Follow the bike trail toward Downtown Cincinnati. Pass through Turkey Ridge Park, the Ohio River will come into view.

(Approx. 5 miles)

DOWTOWN CINCINNATI (S5)

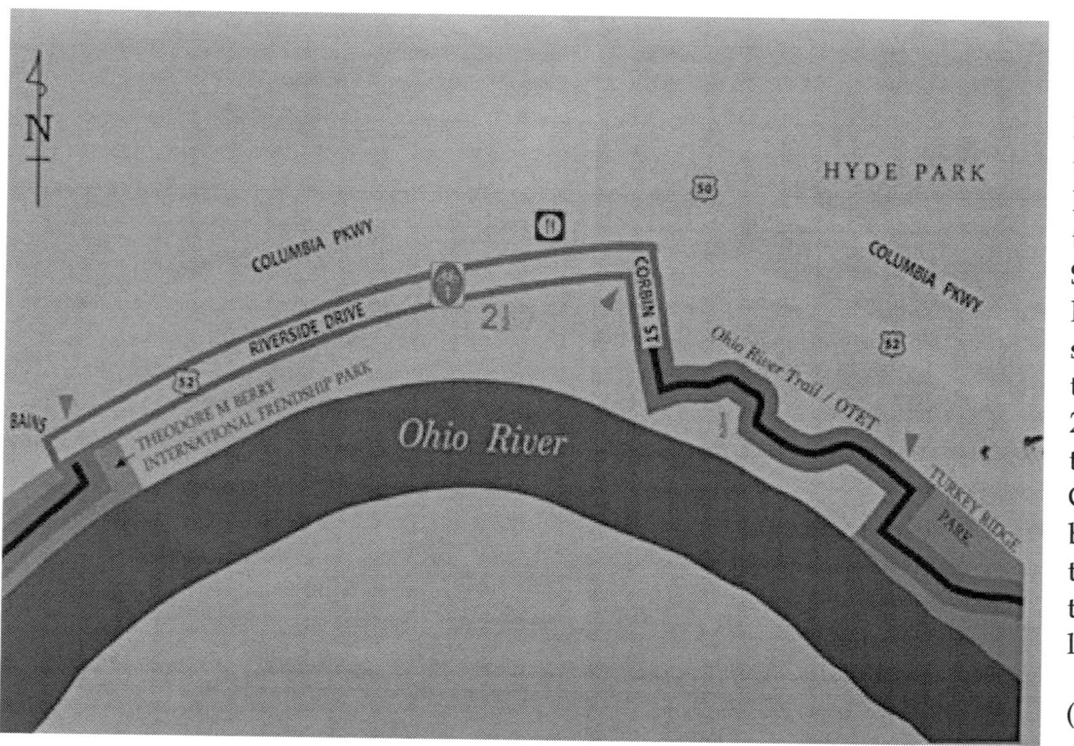

(East to West)

Follow the OTET through Turkey Ridge Park. The trail ends at Corbin Street with a westerly turn onto Riverside Drive. Pick up the Bike path after 2.5 miles and continue to Downtown Cincinnati. You will be with in view of the Ohio River and the Cincinnati skyline.

(Approx. 3 miles)

DOWTOWN CINCINNATI SOUTH TRAIL HEAD (S6)

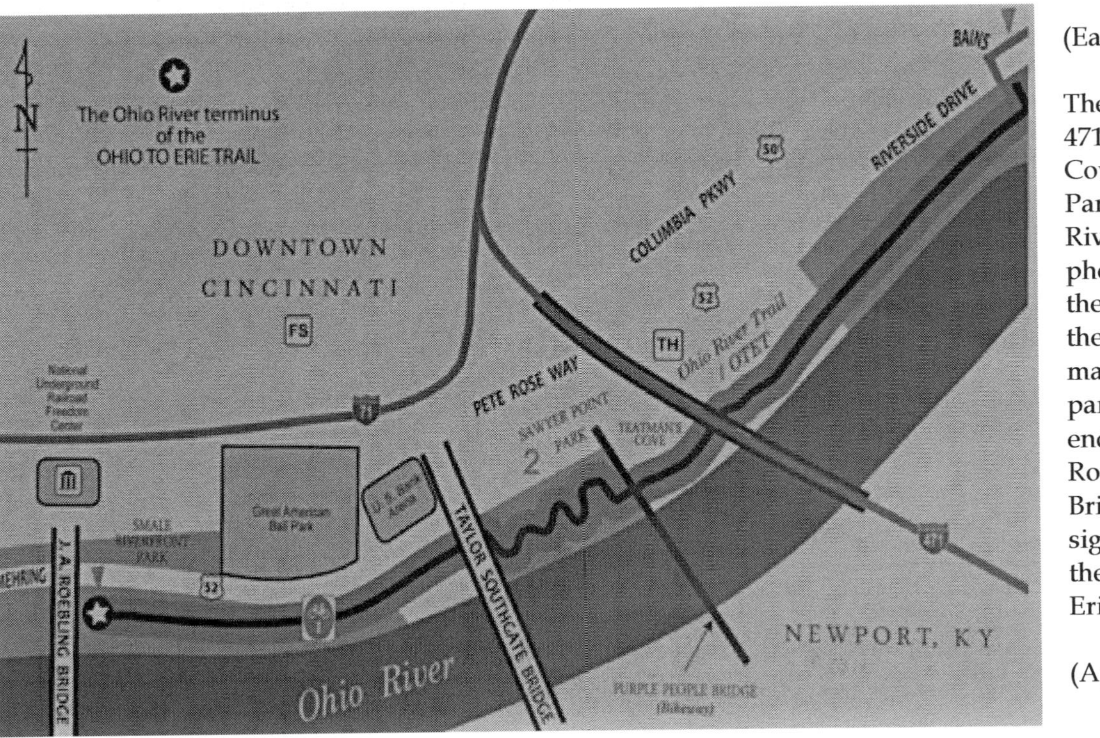

(East to West)

The OTET goes under I-471 past Yeatman's Cove and Sawyer Point Park along the Ohio River. There are great photo opportunities at the Ohio River's edge in the parking lot of Yeatman's cobble stone parking lot. The OTET ends at the blue Roebling Suspension Bridge in Smale Park. A sign in Smale Park tells the story of the Ohio to Erie Trail.

(Approx. 2 miles)

Appendix Three

List of Ohio Historical Markers along the OTET (From Cleveland to Cincinnati, OH)

The Ohio State Historical Society, and Friends of Freedom Society began the state marker program in 1950 which serves to raise awareness of significant people, places and events in Ohio's past. Today there are over 1600 markers throughout the state. The Following list of markers can be found on or near the OTET or State Bike Route One. This list is in order of travel as described in *A Path Through Ohio,* from Cleveland to Cincinnati and north to Troy. The descriptions were obtained and summarized from the actual marker with additional detail found at remarkableohio.org.

110-18 West Side Market (1979 25th St. Cleveland) Is the oldest operating market in Cleveland, dating back to 1909. It is on the National Register of Historic places.

80-18 South Park Village and Whittlesey Tradition (Independence, Cuyahoga County) A four-acre Native America Indian settlement occupied between A.D 1000 and 1600 along the banks of the Cuyahoga River.

1-76 Ohio Erie Canal, Lock Number 4 (Canal Fulton, Stark County) The Erie Canal was in operation by 1832 and represents a series of 142 locks, along a 308 mile stretch, terminating in Lake Erie to the north and the Ohio River to the south. Lock Four is one of the best-preserved examples along the OTET.

73-25 St. Patrick Church (280 N Grant Ave, Columbus) Is the second oldest Roman Catholic Church in Columbus, dedicated in 1853. Was built because of arriving Irish immigrants leaving their country during the Great Famine.

27-25 Camp Chase (2900 Sullivant Ave. Columbus) Civil War Camp established in 1861 was initially developed as a training camp for 150,000 Union soldiers and later converted to a prison camp for 25,000 Confederate soldiers. A cemetery remains to honor the fallen during internment. This historic marker and the cemetery are near the OTET bike path.

47-25 Big Darby Little Darby Creeks (Georgesville, Battelle Darby Creek Metro Park) is a Federally Designated National Scenic River that boast's more than 100 native fish species and 40 fresh water mollusks. Some of these are on the endangered species list.

2-42 Little Indian Fields (Mount Vernon, Knox County) Named for Native American Indians who originally occupied this area along the Kokosing River. The land in this area was later purchased by John "Appleseed" Chapman, who planted the first of many apple orchards in the region around 1809.

9-21, Stage Coach Station, (Sunbury, Delaware County) In 1816 Lawrence Myers, the towns founder anticipated a large increase in stage coach traffic and determined to build an inn at the intersection of Walhonding Trail and the Delaware Newark Pike. In 1820, Sunbury saw its first stage coach which received guests including William Henry Harrison and Rutherford B. Hayes. By 1873 OTET, Cincinnati) was established in 1831. The system used two

Sunbury saw its last stage coach as the rail industry soon replaced the utility of the former mode of travel.

Alum Creek (Sunbury Road, Westerville, Franklin County) 58 miles of this waterway was used as an escape route by slaves seeking protection from bloodhounds and bounty hunters who were tracking their re-capture. Sympathetic residents on Sunbury Road provided shelter and protection along this route which later became known as the Underground Railroad.

10-29 Galloway House (Xenia, Greene County) James and Rebecca Galloway were early pioneers building a Log Cabin in 1799 along the Little Miami River near what is now Goes Station on US Route 68. Galloway was a hunter for soldiers during the American Revolution and later as the first treasurer for Greene County. His son later became the first County surveyor. Rebecca taught noted Indian, Tecumseh the English language through bible study. (Marker is not on the OTET but is located at the Greene County Historical Society Museum)

10-29 Xenia Tornado, April 3, 1974 (Xenia, Greene County) A devastating tornado touched down at 4:40 p.m. killing 34 and destroying hundreds of homes, schools and commercial businesses. (Marker is not on the OTET but is located at the Green County Historical Society Museum)

21-29 First Courthouse (Beavercreek, Greene County) On this site was the first Court house in Greene County. The First proceedings from this log cabin-Court house were held in 1803 and defined the town lines of Beaver Creek.

17-83 Deerfield–South Lebanon (State Route 68, Warren County) Was territory laid out in 1795 as part of American expansion into north western territory. Numerous Revolutionary War and War of 1812 survivors became the early inhabitants of this area.

19-83 Peters Cartridge Co. (1915 Grandin Rd. King Mills, Warren County) Established in 1887 was once a major employer of the area, providing munitions to allied forces during WWI and WWII. Primarily known as a gun powder manufacturer, they later integrated powder packing into shells and casings for ammunition production. Peter's was later purchased by Remington. This site is on US National Register of Historic Places

16-83 Butterworth Station, Underground Railroad (Loveland, Warren County) Also known as the 20-mile house was the southernmost point in Warren County along the Underground Rail road. Hundreds of fugitive slaves found refuge by its owners Benjamin and Rachael Butterworth who were local abolitionists and Quakers. They also donated significant land for the Little Miami Train line which later was recognized as the Butterworth Train station.

Little Miami Railroad (Clermont County) Established in 1863 follows the Little Miami River. In 1860 President Elect Abraham Lincoln rode this line on his way to his inauguration. The line served the area until 1962 and was later converted to pedestrian travel in the 1980's.

42-31 Ohio's first public water system (Near Yeatsman's Cove, steam pumps to draw one million gallons of water per day from the Ohio River.

58-31 Black Brigade of Cincinnati (Near Yeatsman's Cove, OTET, Cincinnati) In September of 1862 Cincinnati was in danger of invasion from Confederate forces in Kentucky. A military battalion-brigade unit of African American citizens was forcibly formed to build defensive fortifications, without fire arms for protection in case of attack. The Brigade would later be known for shouldering their shovels in a military fashion and march in parade formation.

22-31 Cincinnati's German Heritage (Near Yeatsman's Cove, OTET, Cincinnati) First arriving in 1788, then in waves during the 1830's as Cincinnati's booming meat packing industry grew. Again in 1848, due to the Prussian Revolution another wave was experienced. Landmarks of German heritage include, Over the Rhine District, the Roebling Suspension Bridge and the popular Brewing District.

18-31 The Sultana, (Near Yeatsman's Cove, OTET, Cincinnati) One mile from this marker is the site of the John Litherbury Boatyard that built the 260-foot wooden steam transport named the Sultana. On April 27, 1865 the severely over capacitated boat exploded killing over 1200 Union troops returning from the Civil War. Traveling the Mississippi River, near Memphis the boats boilers were unable to meet the demands of a flooded river and overloaded passenger weight, in excess of 1,900. This stands as the worst maritime disaster in American history, and was largely overshadowed due to the killing of John Wilkes Booth, the day before. Additional research by Gene Eric Salecker, Sultana Author.

12-31 French Claims to the Ohio River Valley, (Near Yeatsman's Cove, OTET, Cincinnati) In 1749 French Commander Pierre Joseph Celeron dispatched 250 troops from Montreal to secure territorial claims west of the Allegany Mountains and to protect French interests against the British. Six lead Plates (three of which have been recovered) were placed at the mouths of important tributaries along the Ohio River. One plate was discovered at the mouth of the Great Miami River, not far from this location.

14-31 The Irish in Cincinnati, (Near Yeatsman's Cove, OTET, Cincinnati) a commemoration of the friendship and openness of Cincinnati to receive Irish immigrants during the Great Famine of 1845 and 1850.

Other markers: From Xenia to Piqua On Ohio Bike Route 25

57-9 Site of first NFL game (Dayton)

10-97 Village of Tadmor (Tipp City)

24-25 Miami & Erie Canal Lock 15 (Tipp City)

Appendix Four

Cycle Touring Essentials (for 3 season travel)

Travel by bicycle over greater distances requires a bit more planning than a conventional group ride or single day ride. Your enjoyment and comfort of getting from point A to point B depends on your awareness and preparation for a variety of conditions and concerns. The following tables of advice are prepared to identify the most frequent conditions that have been experienced over many miles of bike travel. Feel free to add or modify these lists based on your individual experiences.

The Ten Essentials

1. Directions: Maps (state, local, trail views), compass, GPS.
2. Water: Two bottles minimum and a way to purify (if needed). *Refill* at every opportunity.
3. Reserve food: High-energy bar, jerky, trail mix, dried fruit & nuts.
4. Clothing: Wicking layer, thermal layer, shell layer.
5. First Aid: (basic) Ointment, aspirin, petroleum jelly, diaper rash cream, sanitizer, band-aids.
6. Mechanical: Multi-purpose tool, tire irons, chain tool, knife, spare inner tube.
7. Lighting: Front & rear lighting, spare headlamp as a backup.
8. Shelter: Vented three-season tent.
9. Sleep gear: Sleeping bag & pad.
10. Prevention: Sunscreen, bug repellant, body cream.

Other Essentials

- Eye protection: Sunglasses.
- Helmet: Properly fitted.
- Eating utensils: Plate, cup, spork (combination spoon & fork), bowl, scrubber.
- Toiletries: Toilet paper, soap, toothpaste, toothbrush, washcloth, towel, hand sanitizer. Include other items as you require.
- Cooking equipment: Lighter, wet-proof matches, stove, fuel, small cook pot set.
- General adventure equipment: Small roll of utility tape, permanent marker, 25-foot parachute chord, 8-inch zip ties, whistle, mirror & plastic garbage bag.

Things to Prepare

- Mechanically sound bike including spokes, chain, brakes, trued wheels, tires, and lubrication.
- Properly loaded panniers that are balanced front and back and side-to-side. Two panniers in back. (Two panniers in the front of the bike are optional based on travel duration). Pack for three changes of clothes if traveling for longer than a week.
- Gear weight: Estimate 35-50 lbs. depending on size or person, duration of trip, and accessory selection.
- Electronics: Portable battery charger (for when power is inaccessible), charge cord, waterproof bag.
- Essentials to be kept accessible: First aid, rain gear, fire starter.
- Keep dry: Sleeping bag, clothing layers, hat and gloves.
- Ride gear: Two changes each: shorts, shirt, socks (alternate and wash), walk-able bike shoes.
- Travel gear: (street clothes) one each of pants, shirt, sneakers, socks.

Things to Know/Remember

- Physical limitations: Overall fitness & limitations, dietary, medical, allergies. Plan on taking walk breaks every 20 miles or after an hour of saddle time.
- First-aid skills: Priority of administering first aid & ABC (Airway, Bleeding, Circulatory).
- Orienteering skills: Maps/compass, GPS. Know where you are & where you're going.
- Local dangers: Poisonous/dangerous animals, plant life, traffic, road shoulder condition.
- Geographical challenges: Mountains, water resources, ferries, bridges, and country borders/passport requirements.
- Weather conditions: Take shelter as necessary. Hypothermia in the summer is a real concern during inclement conditions.
- Civilization checkpoints: Anticipate cities, highways, avoid congestion & high-use roads.
- Three layer clothing system: Wicking, thermal, vented shell.
- Base food: On longer rides each rider should keep a spare soup/oatmeal package for at least two meals for emergency issues. Keep mixed nuts, dried fruit in reserve. There are numerous options for sport bars & gel's if desired.
- Financial considerations: Credit card, cash, exchange rates, & back-up plan.

Community Gear

(for groups larger 2)

- Stove and fuel: Fire-starting items.
- Cooking gear: Pots, large spoon, knife, can opener, cutting mat.
- Food supply as per travel plan.
- Tarp & poles (if you anticipate inclement weather).

Things To Do

- Designate a contact person who will know where you are going & your expected return time.
- Prepare a travel plan with group or contact person, establish checkpoints, exchange phone numbers, and notify authorities as required.
- If you become lost: S.T.O.P. - Stop, Think, Observe, Plan.
- Observe basic personal cleanliness routines. Cleanliness promotes good hygiene and positive attitude for the next day's ride. (Wet towel wipes to a warm shower).
- Be visible on the road using lights, reflectors, vest, flags & clothing.
- Use proper hand signal and audio pronouncements: "car back, on your left, passing, stopping, slowing, clear left/ clear right".

Low Impact (ethical) Camping

- Follow local guidelines.
- Stove cooking only no open fires.
- Get permission on private or restricted property.
- Do not litter. Leave site cleaner than when you arrived.
- Stay on the trail, don't cut the switchbacks.
- Give right-of-way to uphill, motorized vehicles & *wild* animals.
- Camp at least 200 feet from established waterway & other campsites.
- Avoid high ridges, riverbeds or other dangerous locations.
- Avoid digging trenches or rearranging fragile terrain.
- Remove food from tents at night by stringing food up.

Appendix Five
Looney's Road Rules

Road Rule Number One: Start every day with a song.

"Begin the day with a friendly voice, a companion unobtrusive, plays that song that's so elusive, And the magic music makes your morning mood" (Rush, Permanent Waves).

I am a big fan of starting each day with the right attitude in order to gain peak performance from my body. Whether it is the ride into the office or shaking off last night's thundershower while holed up in a tent, the new day brings opportunities to meet new people or to explore one of earth's treasures. As any good athlete prepares for an event, the warm-up is the tool of choice to stretch the body and warm the muscles in preparation for the event. Similarly, the mind needs to warm up. Positive platitudes, visualization exercises, and music are the brain's favorite tools for programming. Although we're not all athletes, starting the day with a positive outlook allows the rider to hop on that saddle just one more time, shake off that cold morning chill, and start churning those pedals to the cadence of a familiar drum beat.

I once had the opportunity to watch the Team USA sprinters warm up for the day's practice at the US Olympic Training Center in Chula Vista, California. From a distance, I watched them jog through their drills on the 400-meter track. At the near end of the beautifully surfaced track was a five-story tower that supported a viewing box and a significant speaker system. As the sprinters concluded their warm-up drills, one came to the tower and blared two audio tracks. The first was a tape from an Olympic stadium with crowd noise as background and the other was the runner's favorite rap music. Inspired by this music, the team went to work immediately.

Road Rule Number Two: Make a journal entry daily.

"There are a thousand thoughts lying within a man that he does not know till he takes a pen to write." William Thackeray.

Summarize each day by making a conscious effort to capture the day's highlights or possibly the low points, the associated feelings, and the key learning. "Hell, I'll never do that again" may be just the note needed to prevent you from repeating the same mistake over. Each is a gem of an emotion to be recalled at a later point in time.

Journal writing in the privacy of your own space allows for free-flowing thoughts to be captured and, if desired, articulated more creatively at a later point. Surprisingly, some of my best moments of self-discovery and observation occur after a long day in the saddle with dinner in the tank and the evening sun fading on the horizon. Take the time to jot, draw, or scribble your likes and dislikes, how you felt, or maybe even a new bucket list idea. As Victor Frankl, a Holocaust survivor once wrote, "Writing allows us to free ourselves from our history". In part, I think he was trying to convey that the simple act of documenting our feelings allows us to move on in life to enjoy or suffer new feelings, making for a richer life experience.

Road Rule Number Three: Sleep with one eye open.

"You must stop and turn to face the dragon, to realize he is made of paper" (Chinese Proverb)

In today's world of verbal diarrhea on TV and bad news which sells best, our society is swept into a condition of fear; fear of walking the dog around the block; fear to go to the "east side" or "that" place. Fortunately, the cyclist does not run into this amped shock culture very often. For some, their fears are more founded in urban

America rather than the woods of rural America.

Yes, there are bears and deer and other wild critters out there that forage for food at night. In our mind's eye, we have a tendency to explode the snapping of a twig or a hearty snort of a buck as a threat and imminent danger that may be lurking in the dark. "Sleeping with one eye open" simply means to be aware of your surroundings and take appropriate precautions. Remove your food from your tent, don't camp near animal feces or tracks, and stay away from freshly dug holes or hollowed timber. Finally, when you first begin camping, you will likely only get partial sleep through most of your camp nights. These fears generally pass as your confidence grows with your capabilities and surroundings. The camping part of adventure cycling is not for everyone. Consequently, there are many reasonable options to pursue. Plan ahead. Make sure your accommodations are confirmed the day before you arrive. Get cleaned up and sleep well. You will have the same challenges the next day as those who chose the ground upon which to sleep.

I have the greatest regard for those who have responded to the call of adventure. Those of you who have experienced this form of travel will likely attest that there is a vast network of bike shops that exhibit a general openness to help a fellow traveler. You're never really alone. The sandbox in which you play is just a little larger than most others.

Road Rule Number Four: For every hill, there is an equal and opposite hill.

Having logged thousands of miles on bike and on foot, I have learned not to fight or become obsessed with the topography and the elements that Mother Nature and fate have put in my path. Standing in frustration at the base of a mountain or staring in the face of dark, foreboding clouds does not change the reality that you must either endure or go home. Rather, be prepared for the extremes and take action in advance to maintain reasonable comfort during tough times. For those of faith, these are the character-enriching experiences that you are in search of. It is God's way of shaping you to use your gifts, turning fear and humility into courage and accomplishment. The silver lining of each experience is that there is a downhill ride and a sunny side to each challenge. Recently, I met another distance cyclist who further characterized this Road Rule—when the wind is at your back make miles, when the wind is at your face take more photographs.

Road Rule Number Five: Know thy food and water needs.

Dietary and hydration concerns are always prevalent when one is exposed to the elements regardless of whether that exposure is just for hours or for trips lasting multiple days. Of the two, hydration is your number one concern in order to maintain proper body fluid levels. I have noticed that the combination of exposure and exercise can best be compensated with up to one liter per hour of water. When urinating, look for a clear fluid as an indication of your success. I also alternate water with sports drinks when on a particularity long grind to help replace lost electrolytes. The calories burned (CB) during a long day's journey is also an important statistic to watch while actively riding. There are many calculators on the Internet that estimate the amount of CB during exercise. I suggest consulting your doctor before embarking on a journey. There are many variables that dictate your physiological needs on a given day. There is much more science behind the maintenance of your physical needs. As you become familiar with any form of distance exercise, be aware of your unique needs and replace calories and fluids regularly. I prefer ice cream any time the opportunity avails itself.

Plan ahead, know the distances between stops and if they are greater than a couple of hours, plan to pack extra reserves. Through force of habit, I generally carry two water bottles and energy bars as a reserve. Let your body be your first indicator to replace fluids and fuel.

Road Rule Number Six: Let go of the electronics, use your surroundings, and use your senses.

"Baby, be a simple, really simple man. Oh, be something you love and understand." Lynyrd Skynyrd, Simple Man

This is not about the resistance to using electronics or popular GPS and experience-enhancing tools. It is about raising your awareness to your experiences. As our technology gets better and better, it also insulates us from our immediate surroundings. It hides in plain sight and can make us oblivious to danger. If you're staring at your GPS, you're losing out not only on the immediate scenery but also may be unaware of that pothole in the road just 10 feet in front of you. Put the watch away. Watches are used for keeping appointments. Some of the best days on the road have a start and end point with the rising and setting of the sun. Allow the entire course of the day to be a series of random and unexpected events.

The last time I checked, your body will tell you when to eat, sleep, and relieve yourself. It's okay to find a park during a midday ride, pull up under a broad-leafed oak to take shelter from the mid afternoon sun, and just take a nap. You're on autopilot now. You may just find that the slice of freedom from your highly structured and complex "other life" is what you have been craving for years.

In case you were wondering, I am old school; maps and compass all the way.

Road Rule Number Seven: Riding alone doesn't mean you're lonesome.

Fellow cyclist Bob Howells once wrote, "When you travel as a group, you're viewed as a group. You're assumed to be collectively self-sufficient. When you're alone, others see you as a fellow human being. People readily share their humanity with you. The earth and the people within unfold in proportion to your openness to them. Each of us has travel preferences that may include solo riding, group riding, or even event riding. The solo option in cycling opens the door to new acquaintances that may change your way of thinking." Road Rule Number Seven is not so much about riding alone as it is about knowing what you want from a ride and how to best achieve these desires. The seasoned traveler may be in search of a new destination such as an unexplored national park. The young adventurer may want to navigate across a trail with GPS and the athlete may want to pound out mega miles; like a hundred miles day. In the end, there is a personal reward for each type of cyclist whether in large groups or as a soloist. Determine your motivations for riding, pick the options that best suit your desired travel, and ride with purpose. The long miles in the saddle will teach you to appreciate your surroundings with all of your senses and challenge you to look into your soul.

Road Rule Number Eight: Know where you are and where you want to be. When in doubt, use multiple maps including state, local or trail.

The obvious reaction to this road rule is to employ the use of a GPS unit. However, many have experienced regions where even the best electronic devices lose reception or experience a blackout. Whether the GPS is your primary or secondary tool for navigation, it is important to know your bearings and to know that you're maintaining the planned trajectory or direction. Learn about the areas through which you will be traveling. Use natural features in your surroundings to keep your bearings correct.

While on a bicycle and generally in congested or urban environments, the need for confirming location checks increases when compared to the speed of a backpacker. There will be numerous challenges for the cyclists attempting to navigate through the congestion of information and traffic. Common mistakes on the cycling road include missed turns, hidden street signs, route numbers for road names, detours, and even good intentions but wrong directions. Each of these challenges can have a potentially disastrous effect. Many years ago in rural Faulkton, South Dakota, I took a turn on an old county road, thinking that I could avoid a strong easterly head wind and later return to my east heading when the wind died down. Though the Triple AAA state maps showed my location and where I ultimately wanted to be, it certainly did not show the conditions I was about to experience along the way. What started as a formal asphalt road deteriorated progressively to the condition of a trail and I soon found myself in a fool's bet. Each reduction in road quality was met with the optimism that this was a temporary degradation and that the traveling surface would surely return to asphalt in the next mile. 20-miles later, my wheels sinking in loose soil and surrounded by corn stalks, I was barely able to see the rooftop of the next farmhouse. Having made a decision to cut my losses, I found a farmer who admired my effort to visit him and he redirected me back down the road I had just traveled. I did return to town in time for lunch after a 40-mile mistake, a much humbled and wiser rider.

So the point of this Road Rule is to use all of the available resources–maps, local people, and GPS. Keep yourself informed to the largest extent possible as to where you are and where you want to be.

Road Rule Number Nine: Embrace your eccentricity.

Everyone has one.
Your mission is to find out what yours is.

It is truly an enlightening sensation to wake up every day in the outdoors with only one purpose–to find out what the day has in store for you. Some days are packed full of stimulation and others are... well... just plain boring. They could be flat, hot, and lacking companionship or they could be just a long, long grind. To the untrained mind, this can be pure torture and, quite honestly, the reason why endurance sport has a bad rap.

When in a rut, I have found a couple of practices to help break up the tedium of long distance riding. The first practice is something I label as associative thinking. Creating a hyper interest and curiosity in every facet of the ride leads to a more efficient performance but also breaks the monotony. Questions that come to mind include monitoring my cadence, miles, speed, ease of breathing, or the distance to the next grocery store. In the meantime, the miles melt away.

The other technique used is known as dissociative thinking. This requires a little creative courage but is equally effective at curing boredom. Your mind is a wonderful tool that can launch a thousand thoughts and emotions from poetic verse to favorite song lyric or a charming line from a movie. When alone on the long, desolate road, you can conjure any rock star you want to be. Go ahead and belt out a couple of favorite tunes. So what if you're off key or miss a word or two. It's the emotion from deep inside tied with the song that brings a rush of feelings. Though I risk dating myself, you may be surprised what comes from your soul, lying just beneath your boredom–possibly a Bob Seger tune or a line from Monty Python and the Holy Grail. For the intellectuals, it could be reciting the Gettysburg Address. Unless you're a karaoke regular, I recommend making sure there's plenty of space between you and anyone in earshot.

Road Rule Number Ten: Always leave a trail of where you've been and where you're going.

In the 2000s, a book titled *Between a Rock and a Hard Place* written by adventurer Aron Ralston describes his survival experience on a rock-climbing trip in Blue John Canyon in Utah. In the course of his trip, his arm became pinched between a sizeable rock formation and a large boulder. Ralston found himself unable to extricate his arm from between the two surfaces. Even worse, he was stuck with limited supplies. The following six days became a gripping tale of survival. Aron later admitted that the whole ordeal could have been avoided if he had just let someone know where he was going and how long he planned to be out of town.

The point here is to keep in touch with someone while striking out on a new adventure. Self-reliance is important for all adventurers but an ounce of preparation such as a compiling a travel itinerary or carrying a charged cell phone can save your hide from the unexpected. By the way, I recommend the book, especially if you're an adrenaline junkie.

Road Rule Number Eleven: Be an ambassador for cycling and be nice to strangers.

In other parts of the world where nomadic travel is a way of life, the traveler is an emissary carrying a message of peace or care for one family or another. In eastern Africa, an old Swahili proverb is commonly used to describe the role of the traveler; "Mgeni aje mwenyeji apone". This roughly translates to "When the guest visits, the host is healed". Many miles of travel have exposed me to those with a dream to be untethered from their life conditions, much as a touring cyclist is untethered from the office chair or work routine. As cyclists, we carry a rare trait of optimism no matter the condition. Yes, we can complain with the best of them but when it comes to enduring distress or physical hardship, the cyclist is equipped like no other. The optimism of the next sunny day, the next farmer's market (and the opportunity to gorge on food), or the next downhill cruise is always around the next corner and often are the stuff of which food dreams are made. With this positive outlook on life, the cycling tourist has a rare opportunity to influence others to experience their surroundings beyond the comfort of a car. The cycling tourist is an ambassador who awakens the possibility that a ride around the block, a ride to the next neighborhood, or a ride across town is achievable. Distant cycling at its core increases the confidence to be self-reliant and go the next mile.

Many years ago while riding through a small farming town in rural Wisconsin, I was coming to the end of a long day with my heavy load on two wheels. I was suddenly startled by a young boy who snuck up behind me on his Stingray bike. He was curious enough to ask, "Where ya going, mister?" As I explained my mission of riding through not just his state but many others as well, he blurted back that he wanted to do that some day. As the chitchat continued over the next couple of miles, we were as close as two kids dreaming about the future from the end of an old, wooden fishing pier. Shortly thereafter, he sped away. Some distance later, I found his bike on the side of the road. The boy and his family were nearby, out in front of their family farm and grocery. As I passed, they waved me down from their front porch and insisted that I select some fresh fruit and cheese from their grocery. This was a small but welcome bonanza for a calorie -craved cyclist. As I walked away from the barn, a faded sign advertising Colby Cheese caught my eye. As I packed up my bike with cheese, I could not help but wonder if this was part of the famed Colby Cheese family.

I don't know if the young rider ever took his Stingray cycling aspirations beyond the family farm but I do know he learned about dreaming big that day.

Road Rule Number Twelve: Stop the negative, replace with positive and realistically assess.

When working with the Boy Scouts as a troop leader, we often ended our long days by sitting around a campfire ring and sharing our thoughts about the day's strenuous hike or other events. This exercise was commonly known as "thorns, rose, and buds ". In turn, each scout would reflect on his likes, dislikes, and most importantly the opportunities that each hoped to see, do, or achieve in the coming days. Surprisingly, even on the most strenuous of days and in the most inclement conditions, each scout could dig deep enough to find one ember of hope that would keep him motivated to move forward.

When performing most physical activities, your mind is assessing your body and its performance. On a surface level, it may be a sore knee or a nagging hitch in a running stride. Each of the day's little events or environmental conditions are also continually being assessed and creating a disposition that can range from euphoric and positive to brooding and negative. Whatever the condition, it is important to be in tune with these changes in mood and outlook.

To stay realistically positive is to recognize the negative elements causing your poor outlook and objectively identify a positive outcome with your available skills and resources. Even when your immediate future looks gloomy, assess all of your skills, your resources, and your equipment when trying to determine a course of action that will lead you to a better outcome. Stay calm and generally unemotional. Think through your options, determine your corrections, and don't procrastinate in taking action.

Road Rule Number Thirteen: Meet someone interesting daily.

Allow conversations to develop.
These are the gems of the day.

When I first biked across the country as a young man, the bike and the travel became a vehicle for seeing national parks and recognizable sights. Looking back after 30-years of travel by bike, I realized that I missed a sizeable portion of self-discovery and purpose for the ride. Replaying the mental tape many years later, the memories that come back in full color are the people that I met and the impressions that they left on me. Don't get me wrong; the photographs and postcard images are all equally beautiful and serene but the brief acquaintances with other human beings carries an emotional context that remains etched in our memory for years afterward.

With many miles of cycle travel behind me, I have experienced highs and lows from each and what I have concluded to be the most memorable achievements are not the places I've been nor the miles I've ridden nor the pain I have endured. The memories most cherished are those that involve human contact and the brief exchange of ideas with people from different backgrounds.

Road Rule Number Fourteen: Dream it - Plan it - Practice it - Do it

Adventure comes in many shapes and sizes and each adventure offers the aspiration to press the limits of physical comfort and mental toughness. Most adventures start as a kernel of an idea influenced by an article in the paper, events that we've encountered in our daily lives, or a challenge laid down by a friend. The kernels are endless. What turns a dream into reality is hard-core planning. This kind of planning accounts for every detail, bringing you closer to a crystalized picture of the target. Planning requires you to take that bold step of converting a "cool idea" into a written statement. As that written statement hangs on your mirror or some other conspicuous location, your mind subconsciously gnaws away at the details. Gradually over time, your plan starts to develop in detail and color. Keep adding detail to your plan until the point where you feel a personal commitment to the plan and can willingly describe it to a friend or confidant. With an internalized commitment and some constructive feedback, you're ready to go to the next phase. Practice it.

While the planning phase allows you to visualize your "Big Hairy Plan" (BHP), the "practice it" phase now consumes your conscious thoughts. You take actions to study route maps, create gear lists, and most importantly, go out and ride for the exercise and mental preparation. All of these actions are building upon your BHP and helping you internalize the vision that you have. During the "practice it" phase, continue to talk to your friends; "Here's what I am thinking, what do you think?" Each conversation continues to build your commitment to the BHP and at the same time sends a signal to the rest of your inner circle of friends, "I'm gonna do this".

After months of planning and preparation, you're now on day one of your BHP. This is the "do it" phase. At this time, you should feel confident that you've put in the hard work of planning and practice. You may feel a little nervous about some detail you missed but by and large, your BHP is solid. As the miles roll along on day one, you will feel an abundance of excitement as the strings of responsibility slip away. And your confidence will continue to grow mile after mile.

Road Rule Number Fifteen: Define your trip goals in advance but be agile enough to change your goals.

The cornerstone of every adventurer is to balance the elation of achievement with the risk of not being successful. Underestimate the risk or overestimate your ability and problems will start to appear. Fortunately, we each have the ability to define the boundaries or goals of our adventure. We also have the ability to change the goal. After all, it is "your goal".

In a prior life as a running/ marathon coach, I prescribed a structured, three-layer goal-setting expectation for each student. In other words; "following a race, what three outcomes from the race would make you feel like you accomplished your mission?" Too many times, we don't carefully think through why we are investing enormous training hours and sacrifices and to what end. The "why am I doing this marathon" gets lost in the busyness of training. I once had a runner who had just completed an admirable marathon and immediately asked, "How did I do, coach?" Trying to get the runner to identify with the deeper meaning of the question, I responded, "How did you think you did?" Though a simplistic example, this runner had not defined a successful outcome and after a couple more questions, this runner felt a little more satisfied with her race. The runner has the opportunity to set goals on many different levels of race performance. As an example, three different outcomes for a goal might be to a) just finish the race or b) finish with a select time in mind or c) finish in the top 10% in an age group. This skill can easily become a valuable tool in defining success for any adventure.

Similar to the runner, the adventure cyclist should establish expectations in a way that defines a successful outcome. In business terms, we call these SMART objectives; Specific, Measurable, Actionable, Realistic, and Time-bounded. A quick Google search on SMART goals will provide a wealth of information on how to establish and manage your trip goals.

A final note on goal setting

As important as it is to define the goals of your adventure, try not to lose sight of the fact that these are self-made and left up for interpretation as the adventure unfolds. There are an unlimited number of events that may cause you to change your goal. Be flexible with your goals to the point that your decisions to change are simply alterations to enhance your safety or experience from the original design. For me, I generally abandon my "daily miles" goal when I meet someone new or interesting. Establish your goals but be flexible enough to modify them as the conditions around you warrant.

Acknowledgements

As most can imagine, the tedious work of producing an body of research and passion into a published book while tending to life's other needs can drag out the progress of completion. To this end, I want to acknowledge those who helped me on my journey. I am grateful to each person who continually coached and prodded my progress.

Contributors:
Laurie Di Giacomo-Looney first on any of my lists is my wife, who helped me to maintain my voice throughout this work. In addition, her continued support through long days of my absenteeism and her willingness to singlehandedly take care of our family while I was out on the road has allowed me to creatively explore the country. Her sometimes critical and always loving view, not only of my eccentricities but also of my commitment to travel and writing, continues to stimulate conversation for us. These conversations resulted in a balanced perspective of what we believe the audience wants to read. At my day job, we call this WIFM, (what's in it for me). Hopefully, you found the WIFM value in reading this book.

Tom Hofbauer served as my editor. His attention to detail and correctness provided a structure to my writing that allowed a conversational story to evolve. Similar to most athletic events, we regularly challenged each other with the goal of shaping this book to be the best that we could produce. Never more than a phone call away; Tom was quick to find solutions to my word blocks.

Susan Mangan, helped mentor and inspire a technical engineer with a penchant for detail to shift from a writing style based on facts and details committed to memory, to one based on sensual observations found in the heart. My transition to creative writing required a leap of faith that may have never happened without Susan's excitement for the written word. It is contagious and unparalleled.

Ohio Department of Natural Resources is the administrative department of the OH state government charged with maintaining natural resources such as state parks, state nature reserves, state wildlife areas, state forests and state waterways. **(www.ohiodnr.gov)**

Ohio To Erie Trail Fund
Ed Honton: (June 5, 1930 -October 12, 2005) **Founder** of the OTET 1991, Founder of the Great Ohio Bike Adventure, GOBA. Franklin County Civil Engineer, President of the Columbus Council of American Youth Hostels.

Jerry Rampelt, Ed Dressler (Green County), Mary Hess, Ellen Tripp, early contributors to the Ohio to Erie Fund.

Wayne Roberts and Gene Pass; "Roberts Pass" Developers of the path section leading into London OH

The 2018 Ohio To Erie Trail, (OTET) Board of Directors*
Bill Daehler, Vice President (Franklin County)
Elizabeth Watts, Treasurer (Franklin County)
Mary Plumley, Secretary (Franklin County)
Lisa Daris, Executive Coordinator
Bruce Bailey (Franklin County)
Wayne Roberts, (Madison County)
Tom Alexander, (Holmes County)
James Flaherty, (Delaware County)
Mike Groeber, (Clark/Greene Counties)
Chris Hadocy, (Franklin County)
Sean McGurr, (Summit County)
Don Mills, (Hamilton County)
Don Noble, (Wayne County)
Jerry Rampelt, (Franklin County)
Dan Ritchey, (Coshocton County)
Bob Taft, (Greene County)
Jack Williams, (Ross County)
Jay Telzrow, (Cuyahoga County)
Ken Schneider, (Cuyahoga County)
**See the OTET website for a current list of Board of Director*

References

Websites

Detailed OTET Tour Guides make your trip planning easy. The entire 326-mile route is divided into four regions with very detailed direction guides. The tour guide is a very detailed set of four maps printed on four sheets of paper that are 8¼ X 25½ and folded to make six panels. All four sheets arrive in a custom plastic envelope making a neat and easy to use navigation kit. Each panel contains a map, mileage and a written.
For Ohio to Erie Trail Maps go to www.ohiotoerietrail.org

Northern Region, map one: Cleveland, Akron, Massillon, Fredericksburg, and Millersburg

North Central Region, map two: Killbuck, Danville, Mount Vernon, Sunbury, and Westerville

South Central Region, map three: Columbus, London, and Xenia

Southern Region, map four: Spring Valley, Loveland to Cincinnati

Ohio to Erie Trail & Miami Valley Bikeway map, courtesy of **Robert Niedenthal.**

Miami Valley Bikeways go to www.miamivalleytrails.org
Provides information about each of the Rail Trails and other multi-use trails centered on Dayton and Xenia.

Print Media

Glaser, Susan (2014, April 22). New Map helps bikers navigate the Ohio to Erie Trail; plus GOBA deadline approaches. Cleveland Plain Dealer. Retrieved from http://www.cleveland.com/travel/index.ssf/2014/04/new_map_helps_bikers_navigate.html
Bob Howell, *Touring Solo*, Bicycle Rider January/February 1986. Print
Allen W. Eckert's *The Frontiersmen.* Ashland: Jessie Steward Foun-

dation, 2001. Print
Peter Jenkins, *A Walk Across America.* New York: Harper Collins Publishers, Inc., 1979. Print
Dan Egan, *The Death And Life Of the Great Lakes.* W.W. Norton & Company, 2017. Print

Selected Music

Rush. *Spirit of Radio.* Mercury Records 1980, Album.
Bob Seger. *Traveling Man.* Capitol 1975, Album
Foreigner. *I Want To Know What Love Is.* Atlantic 1984
John Denver. *Take Me Home, Country Roads.* RCA 1971
Glen Campbell. *Rhinestone Cowboy.* Capitol 1975
Kenny Rogers. *The Gambler.* United Artists 1978
Daryl Hall and John Oates. *Lost that Loving Feeling.* RCA Records 1980
REO Speedwagon. *Keep Pushin.* Epic Records 1977.

Made in the USA
Columbia, SC
27 August 2019